D1042241

HOW TO MAKE
MONEY
WITH
JUNK
BONDS

HOW TO MAKE
MONEY
WITH
JUNK
BONDS

ROBERT LEVINE

NEW YORK   CHICAGO   SAN FRANCISCO
LISBON   LONDON   MADRID   MEXICO CITY   MILAN
NEW DELHI   SAN JUAN   SEOUL   SINGAPORE
SYDNEY   TORONTO

1 2 3 4 5 6 7 8 9 0   DOC/DOC   1 8 7 6 5 4 3 2

ISBN: 978-0-07-179381-0
MHID: 0-07-179381-X

e-book ISBN: 978-0-07-179382-7
e-book MHID: 0-07-179382-8

This publication is designed to provide accurate and authoritative information in regard to the subject matter covered. It is sold with the understanding that neither the author nor the publisher is engaged in rendering legal, accounting, securities trading, or other professional services. If legal advice or other expert assistance is required, the services of a competent professional person should be sought.

—*From a Declaration of Principles Jointly Adopted by a Committee of the American Bar Association and a Committee of Publishers and Associations*

Library of Congress Cataloging-in-Publication Data
Levine, Robert.
    How to make money with junk bonds / by Robert Levine.—1st ed.
       p. cm.
    ISBN 978-0-07-179381-0 (alk. paper)—ISBN 0-07-179381-X (alk. paper)
    1. Junk bonds. 2. Capital market. 3. Investments. I. Title.
    HG4651.L48 2012
    332.63'23—dc23   2012000544

McGraw-Hill books are available at special quantity discounts to use as premiums and sales promotions, or for use in corporate training programs. To contact a representative, please e-mail us at bulksales@mcgraw-hill.com.

This book is printed on acid-free paper.

CONTENTS

FOREWORD

BY MARTIN S. FRIDSON

This is a great book by a great investor. It is not by any means the first one ever written about high yield bonds. Some of the early books did not offer advice on investing in high yield bonds, but instead they focused on the controversies surrounding their use in hostile takeovers during the 1980s. Several others published since then were aimed at institutional investors, rather than individuals desiring to buy high yield mutual fund shares or to create their own portfolios.

Now, at last, there is a nuts-and-bolts book for nonprofessional investors hoping to capitalize on the unique advantages of speculative grade debt. No one is better qualified to write such a book than Bob Levine. Not only is he a master of the principles of high yield credit analysis, but he also played a major role in establishing them.

In the early days of the market, "story bonds" was a frequently heard phrase. The term usually signified that the issuing company's financials were none too good, so the salesperson attempting to peddle the bonds hoped buyers would be persuaded by a little razzle-dazzle. Bob was in the forefront of analysts who insisted on greater rigor in high yield valuation, and as head of a high yield asset management business, he helped push underwriters to a higher standard. At the same time, Bob always remembered that numbers do not tell the whole story; it is essential to understand why a company's business is likely to flourish or fail.

Readers of *How to Make Money with Junk Bonds* are fortunate to have the benefit of Bob Levine's experience. I am even more fortunate to have known him for 30 years. During that time he has been a competitor, a client, a colleague in professional organizations, and that for which I am proudest—a friend. It is therefore a great pleasure to commend this book to everyone who wants to acquire some invaluable horse sense about investing in high yield bonds.

Martin Fridson is the author of *How to Be a Billionaire* and other investment books including those on junk bonds.

FOREWORD
BY JOEL GREENBLATT

Like most people just getting started in their hoped-for career, I needed a break. It was 1979, I was all of 21 years old (please refrain from doing any calculations), and I was trying to get my first toehold on Wall Street. I was up for a summer job in the research department of the venerable firm of Kidder, Peabody & Company, and I was being interviewed by one of its young vice presidents. Getting this job meant a lot to me because in each interview at every firm, the interviewers had kept asking for my prior Wall Street work experience, and, of course, I had none. This was the sort of vicious circle that almost everyone faces at the beginning of his or her career.

I had only two edges. First, the stock market hadn't gone up over the prior 11 years, and Wall Street wasn't exactly the most popular place to look for a job at the time. Second, and clearly more important, the young vice president who sat across the table was Bob Levine. In a lucky break for me, Bob was interested only in the way I thought about things, not my Wall Street experience. I guess he already knew way back then that he was a great teacher. He was just looking for the right kind of student. Somehow, I must have passed muster because Bob ended up giving me that critical first chance to show what I could do. Each day for the entire summer, I'd get off the elevator and walk over to tap the Kidder, Peabody sign just to make sure the whole thing was real (or maybe I was being obsessive compulsive—there's such a thin line with these things). But each day for the entire summer, I also had the privilege to benefit from Bob's considerable expertise and from his incredible patience as a teacher. I'll always be grateful.

Now, you too have the chance to benefit from Bob's abilities as a teacher. To be a good investor, you must have understanding. You have to have a deep understanding of the process and a great road map leading you to your goals because there will always be times when your investments are not working out. The only way to stick it out during those tough times is to understand what you are doing. Bob is a junk bond expert, and there's a lot of money to be made in this area. With decades of success behind him, Bob knows this firsthand in a big way. The important thing is that he is now willing to share this knowledge and experience with you.

And he does it incredibly well. This book is clear, insightful, and written in a simple manner so that diligent readers can learn and actually gain the understanding necessary to have a great deal of success in the junk bond (aka high yield bond) field. Few experts in this area have been willing to share their inside knowledge with the outside world. None have done it as well and as simply and clearly as Bob Levine has done in his new book.

Read it. Enjoy it. Learn from it. And after you're done with it, if you have some success, please remember to come over every once in a while and tap the cover to display your appreciation (or serious anxiety disorder).

Joel Greenblatt is the author of *The Little Book That Beats the Market, The Little Book That Still Beats the Market,* and *The Big Secret for the Small Investor.*

Acknowledgments

There are many people I would like to thank for helping me with this book. Friends, former colleagues, and especially my family have been extraordinarily supportive. In particular, I would like to thank the people at my former company Nomura Corporate Research and Asset Management (NCRAM); they are talented, brilliant, and nice people. In particular, I want to thank David Crall whom I have worked with for nearly 20 years since he graduated from college. Over the years he has advanced from student, to employee, to partner. David's advice and examples were extraordinarily helpful to the preparation of this book. In addition, I would like to thank others at NCRAM including Steve Kotsen, Steve Rosenthal, Josh Givelber, Maryana Kushnir, Eve Drucker, Amy Yu, and the whole high yield team. While I initially hired and trained them, I learned more than I taught, and their suggestions and examples were critical to the writing of this book and the success of NCRAM. I would like to thank Professor Frank Reilly of Notre Dame University for his insight and advice, particularly for Chapters 6 and 12.

I am grateful to Debbie Montick and Tony LaCivita for their help in organizing my thoughts and their editing suggestions. Debbie's sage advice and criticism of my writing style and rewriting of certain pages enormously helped the readability of this book. Tony's line-by-line comments and reorganization ideas were terrific. Special thanks to Noah Gaynor who was an early partner. Noah epitomizes the theory that if you give young people responsibility, their intelligence and energy will be astounding. His advice on the text and his computer skills made this book possible. Also, thanks to Frank Fulginiti and Mike Tipermas who took over for Noah and helped me finish the book.

I would like to thank Nomura for allowing me to use the high yield track record in this book. This book could not have been written with such great examples without the terrific information provided by the research and index teams of J.P. Morgan and Merrill Lynch. Merrill's index team provides a great value to the high yield market. Peter Acciavatti and his group at J.P. Morgan provided excellent high yield research that was invaluable to the completion of this book.

The help and encouragement of my editor Mina Samuels, and especially my literary agent Sandra Dijkstra, made this whole process enjoyable. Thank you also to Martin Fridson and Joel Greenblatt for writing the forewords. Joel and I worked together at the beginning of his career, and he has gone on to do great things. Marty and I have been friends and competitors since the 1980s, and he is one of the great professionals in the high yield industry.

I would also like to thank my three children, Adam, Molly, and Matthew, for their encouragement and my loving wife, Judy, for her advice with this book and for her love and support.

INTRODUCTION

For many investors, the junk bond market is obscure and complex—an asset class to avoid. After all, goes the logic, a market sector termed "junk" can't be healthy for the untrained layperson. Further, a market with predominantly "institutional" players can't be a safe place for even sophisticated retail players. Yet, companies that issue junk bonds, also known as high yield bonds, pervade investors' lives and portfolios.

Many companies issuing junk bonds are the very companies that investors would not hesitate to own the public equity outright or as part of a conservative mutual fund portfolio. You know the names: General Motors (the automotive giant bailed out by the U.S. government); Cablevision (the cable provider predominant in the New York–Long Island area); Sprint Nextel Corporation (the large wireless and wireline telecom company); or Harrah's (Caesars Entertainment, the gaming and hospitality corporation). Bond prices affect stock prices of a company, so learning about the bonds will help you invest in the stock of the same companies. An understanding of the pitfalls, liabilities, and utility of junk bonds will enhance your ability to identify strong companies and may ultimately give you the courage to jump into the junk bond market.

This book is about picking junk bonds to invest in, written from an insider's view. I have been an analyst, a portfolio manager, chief investment officer, and president of a junk bond asset management company. From October 1991 when I started building the junk bond asset management business at Nomura Securities until January 2010 when I left, our junk bond return was a cumulative 695%[1] compared to 364%[2] for the market as defined by the Bank of America Merrill Lynch benchmark for high yield bonds. This was nearly twice the market return over the many up and down markets that we experienced. How did I accomplish this?

Over the years, I have developed a method to pick the correct investments; that method is called Strong-Horse Investing. My Strong-Horse Investing Method has provided above average returns to individual and institutional investors over the long term by focusing on certain key factors about companies while acknowledging trends in the market. Strong-Horse Investing is a way of picking high yield bonds that have a low possibility of default. A Strong-Horse company is one whose strength of operations can support a heavy debt burden. This book teaches you how to identify Strong-Horse companies, that is, those worth investing in.

At 35 years old, the junk bond market is a much less rough-and-tumble place than the one I encountered in my early days as an analyst at the former Wall Street powerhouse Kidder, Peabody. At that time, in my opinion, there was a chain of abuses as a result of a near Drexel monopoly. Issuers and deals were brought to market that could not be accepted in today's more transparent setting. Information about the market is also more easily accessible for investors now. We have an established high yield corporate bond market that pays a higher coupon for a higher risk, and many underwriters have junk bond departments.

Junk bonds have become an important sector of the securities market. More important, investing in the current junk bond market demands careful and thorough analysis mixed with some derring-do and risk taking, and, of course, a dash of intuition. But the rewards are compelling.

In this book, I stay away from discussing expensive computer platforms that provide a wealth of information to the institutional community. You do not need such minute-to-minute pricing or other data for successful investing. The SEC databases are a terrific resource: they are up to date and free. In fact, these databases are the source of a good deal of price information for more expensive vendors. In this book, I show you how to access that information.

We will delve into when it makes sense to own stock or extend credit, how to evaluate the risks of a business, and how to employ a tried-and-true method of making money by lending to high-risk businesses with a potential to generate strong returns. It is not difficult to do, but it requires hard work on occasion and a belief that over the long term, the debt markets are logical.

My journey has not been without incident. Over the years, I have learned about serial defaulters—these are industries, companies, managers, and owners who keep coming back to sell junk bonds despite horrendous records of failure. And so, you will learn how to distinguish between the good, the bad, and the ugly. But in the end, you too will know how to find those strong, agile, and forward-looking companies in the junk bond market that not only know how and when to grow, expand, and flourish but also how to avoid market pitfalls that have destroyed other ongoing concerns and competitors. To reach the goal of investing in junk bonds successfully, I cover the following:

- *The difference between stocks and bonds:* Junk bonds fit between stocks and bonds along the risk spectrum.

- *The importance of a thorough credit analysis:* This is the key to making money in this market.

- *How to evaluate market conditions:* There are times to invest, and there are times to sit on the sidelines.

- *The need for a portfolio manager and how to select the best one for you.*

- *How to avoid common mistakes:* I use some real-life examples.

- *How to invest like a professional:* You will have the benefit of my experience when you finish reading the book.

CHAPTER 1

JUNK BONDS AND STRONG HORSES

Greece does it; so does General Motors. So do Gannet and Goodyear Tire.

What do they all have in common besides names that start with the letter *G*? They all issue junk bonds.

Junk bonds are not the scary or second-rate securities their name evokes. They are not the bond equivalent of penny stocks (thinly capitalized start-ups that, more often than not, flame out). Their reputation is worse than the reality: junk bonds often provide a higher return to investors than their investment grade brethren. The companies discussed in this book are all real companies whose stock you might own.

The extent to which junk bonds are central to the U.S. capital market is surprising to most people. According to J.P. Morgan, the junk bond market is huge: over $1 trillion. There are more than 1,000 junk bond issuers. Many of these companies also issue public stock. The bonds of these companies are attractive investment alternatives to the stocks for two reasons: First, the bonds typically provide a steady stream of interest income to the maturity date. Second, in the event that a company faces financial stress, the bonds are senior to the equity (stocks) so the investor has a greater chance to recover on an investment. Many sophisticated pension funds, both state and corporate, have allocated substantial money to this sector. Junk bonds can also enhance portfolio returns.

Junk bonds are debt securities issued by a corporation that has been rated below investment grade by the major rating agencies. When I talk about this market, I will use three terms interchangeably: *junk, high yield,* or *speculative grade bonds.* Generally, these bonds have higher yields, between 2% and more than 10% above the risk-free rate of U.S. Treasury bills, and they have a higher failure rate than higher-rated bonds. They are issued by many companies, including those that are well established and play a significant role in the U.S. economy.

You may wake up on a Sealy mattress, shower with Selsun Blue (Chattem Corp.), or brush your teeth with toothpaste bought at a Rite Aid. Hungry? You may have cereal purchased at a SUPERVALU or an A&P or the Pantry. Do you want to put a banana in your cereal? It could be delivered by Chiquita Brands. Juice? Try Del Monte or Dole. Don't want cereal? Go to Denny's for eggs with bacon from Smithfield Foods. To get there, drive in a Chevrolet (General Motors) or a Chrysler or a Ford. Is it cold in your house? Call Public Service of New Mexico. While making that call, use a FairPoint Communications line, or a Cincinnati Bell telephone line, or maybe even a CenturyLink line. Every one of these companies mentioned issues junk bonds.

The airline industry is dominated by junk bond issuers. The telecommunications industry—wireline and wireless— has many junk bond issuers too. The older and most prominent automobile rental companies, Hertz and Avis, issue junk bonds, as do some prominent waste management companies. Retailers such as Dillard's, Ethan Allen, J.C. Penney, Saks Fifth Avenue, Sally Beauty Supply, and Pep Boys are all junk bond issuers. Ever go gambling? If so, it is likely you have played tables at a casino owned by a company that issues junk bonds (the gaming sector is full of them): Boyd Gaming, Las Vegas Sands, the Mirage (MGM Resorts International), Penn National Gaming, and Wynn Resorts. Need medical help? Try junk bond issuers HealthSouth Corp., HCA, Alere, and Tenet Healthcare.

Junk bonds are now part of the investment landscape, and you ought to understand the merits, risks, and returns of this asset class. What follows is my Strong-Horse Investing Method for navigating through this market. I also discuss the junk bond advantage and some potential problems to avoid.

The Strong-Horse Method is value investing for bonds in which a credit analysis of a corporation is performed for the purpose of calibrating how strong or weak the company's financials are. I relate that calibration to the price the bonds should trade at and look for what I perceive to be market inefficiencies. I call this Strong-Horse Investing because it describes the image of the type of company I look for when investing in junk bonds. A company with a powerful business that is a market share leader and low cost producer. A Strong-Horse company is in control of its future and able to generate excess cash flow to pay down debt over time and spend for the future. Such a company has a competent and ethical management team and ownership structure. Importantly, its sales and profits are rising, and it does not have too much debt. Finally, the value of the company must be worth more than the debt it has on its books.

CHAPTER 2

MY SON'S FRIEND MILLIE

Riding a bicycle and carrying a messenger bag, my son's friend Millie weaves around town delivering packages and letters for a fee. Millie is the talk of the town, always with money for the movies as well as a bag of popcorn; she enjoys an active social life. Millie is in fat city. She makes $10 a day, five days a week, for half of the year. She works only half of the year because the weather is too bad to ride her bike during the other half. Therefore, her revenue is $1,300 per year. Unfortunately the bike is old and frequently breaks down. Millie is afraid that if she cannot fix her bike, she will lose customers. She can make only two deliveries per day, but sometimes she has the demand for three or four. So many people want her service that she may want to buy a second bike and hire a second rider. A new bike costs $200, and a bike repair costs $100.

Millie has asked my son to lend her $300 to both fix the old bike and buy a new one. My son is afraid that if he lends her the money, Millie may not repay him or she may take too long to repay him. Millie does not know how to work on bikes herself, and she always has to take them to the shop to be fixed. Getting her bike fixed takes time, and she may lose customers since she won't be able to make deliveries while her bike is in the shop. Millie may not have enough new customers to justify the cost of buying a second bike. She also faces the risk that her new employee will simply run away with the bike. Currently, my son is holding his money in an interest-bearing account in the bank, meaning he has *opportunity costs*. If Millie doesn't pay him something for the use of the money, he is actually losing money himself—the interest from that bank account.

My son needs to figure out how long it will take Millie to repay him so that he can determine whether a loan is worth making. Let's say that Millie makes $5 per delivery and that she makes two deliveries a day. If she keeps this up, she should be able to pay my son back in 30 business days ($10 × 30 days = $300):

- If she gets a second bike, she must hire someone to make those extra deliveries. Millie decides to post an ad in the classifieds for a bike messenger position at a wage of $5 per day.

- If the new messenger makes two deliveries in a day, Millie will make $5 ($10 from deliveries − $5 wage = $5).

- However, if the new messenger makes only one delivery in a day, Millie will not make any money. Instead, she will break even ($5 from deliveries − $5 wage = $0).

- Further, if the new messenger has no delivery requests in a day, she will lose $5 because she will still have to pay him for idly waiting for messenger requests ($0 from deliveries − $5 wage = −$5).

My son must also weigh the competitive nature of Millie's business. With no barriers to entry, anyone with a functional bike could easily enter the bike messenger market, cutting into Millie's business and customer base. Are new competitors entering the bike messenger market? Will a new rider start his own messenger company, competing with Millie?

Although my son views Millie as diligent and hardworking, he wants to get his money back. He wants to determine what Millie's demand will be like in the coming weeks. He needs to consider the business lost due to inclement weather and/or maybe even lost customers. These are all factors he must consider in order to make an educated analysis as to whether he will receive his money back.

The bank is currently offering my son 2% (or $6 on his $300) to keep his money in the bank for one year. That money has no risk while the bank has it because the federal government is guaranteeing his money. Millie is willing to pay him 3%, or $9, but her offer has all the risks mentioned. My son is fond of Millie, but he isn't sure if the extra $3 is worth the risk of lending her the money.

Millie's story is a simple one, but it provides a framework within which to understand the role of junk bonds in the U.S. capital markets. Buying junk bonds is equivalent to lending money to a company. Throughout this book, we will learn about evaluating the risks of lending. Over the past 30 years, I've loaned billions of dollars to companies at all different risk levels, and it never ceases to amaze me how people ask the wrong questions and make the wrong decisions in the hopes of getting a paltry 1% extra return on their investments. Then, instead of getting that 1% extra return, they often lose their entire investment. Fear and greed rule both the stock and the bond markets, and for that reason, my son did not lend Millie the money.

Now come with me as we take a ride in the high yield corporate bond market. We will learn how to invest in this ever-more-important capital market—it is not hard to do, and I will keep the material at a basic level. By following these concepts, you can make money over the long run. I'll introduce people who have defaulted many times and lost money for their investors many times but also others who have been upstanding citizens and have provided valuable returns to their investors. By the end of this book, you will be able to determine if my son made the right decision to not lend Millie the money, but more important, you will know how to best put your money to use. So let's get started.

· WHAT WE KNOW ·

1. Lending involves risk.

2. As a lender, do not be greedy and take on unusually high risk for a small extra return.

3. Millie is a young entrepreneur with a good future. She may eventually go into private equity.

CHAPTER 3

My Son's Graduation Money

A few years have passed since my son declined to lend Millie $300. He has just graduated from college, and he has received a gift of $1,000. He wants to do something with the money and has listed his options.

He is interested in traveling to Fort Lauderdale, Florida, for vacation. After four years of studying hard in college, this option is very attractive to him. The water is perfect, the sand is great, and there are many interesting activities to take part in during the day and, especially, at night. He could book a Starwood Hotel room, get on a Continental Airlines flight, and party it up on the beach (both Continental and Starwood are junk bond issuers). While using his time and money to take the trip has some merit, there are other viable options in which to invest. Let's explore some of them.

The first investment option is to take very little risk and put the money in cash or a cash equivalent, such as a short-term Treasury bill, a bank savings or checking account, or a money market fund. These options (particularly a money market fund or a bank) have merit if my son wants easy access to his money or if he wants absolute safety (as he would have with a federally guaranteed T-bill). There is virtually no chance of losing any of his money, and he'll have ready access to it when he wants it. Say, for example, he decides to go to Florida next spring, and he wants to have additional money at that time. Unfortunately, next spring his money still will be worth $1,000. He will not have earned anything on that $1,000, and one year later it will be worth the same amount, or less if there have been fees to pay. Nevertheless, the federal government will see to it that his bank deposit and T-bill are safe. While money market funds are not as safe as bank accounts and T-bills, they are sufficiently safe for our purposes here, so we will assume they are. At the time of this writing, there is virtually no return for bank deposits, T-bills, and money market funds. We will assume that the risk-free rate is 0%. (This rate is subject to change as the economy fluctuates.)

One year from now, due to inflation, my son's $1,000 vacation may cost $1,100. In that case, my son won't be able to afford the trip. (This is a problem because Millie is planning a vacation in Fort Lauderdale next year, and my son wants to spend time with her.)

The second option my son has is to invest his graduation money in corporate bonds. A *corporate bond* is debt incurred by a corporation for the purpose of expanding its business and funding its *dividends*—that is, the regular payments it makes to its shareholders. Essentially, a company borrows money from investors when it wants to grow its business in some way or pay a dividend to shareholders. The company then pays the lenders or investors interest on the capital it has borrowed.

Corporate bonds can be further categorized to make it simpler for investors to understand the perceived health of a company. Less risky bonds are called *investment grade bonds*, while riskier bonds are known as *high yield bonds* or *junk bonds*. In today's market my son could earn 4%, or $40, interest by investing in investment grade bonds. While this type of investment is riskier than a T-bill or money market fund, it will still not generate enough return to achieve my son's goal.

As we know, junk bonds are corporate bonds that carry a higher return along with a greater risk of *defaulting*—not paying back debt. Today my son may earn 10%, or $100, interest by taking on this risk. Unfortunately, this may be more risk than he wants.

My son's final option is to invest the $1,000 in *equities* (via the stock market), which is simply buying a share or shares of a company. If there are more buyers than sellers, the price of his shares will increase; and in reverse, if there are more sellers than buyers, the price of his shares will decrease. Unfortunately, the value of equities can go down as well as up based on the outlook and prospect for the company that issues them. That movement is known as *volatility*. On average, over the past 5-, 10-, and 15-year periods ending March 31, 2010, equities have also earned less than the $100 on a $1,000 investment that my son needs to get to Florida next year.

The options discussed here are just a few of the various Treasury, fixed income (bonds), and equity (stocks) investment products available. My son could select Treasury bonds with varying maturities or mortgage-backed securities, as other fixed income options. For the purpose of this book, we will focus on making money only by investing in corporate bonds. I am not discussing junk mortgage securities or any other low rated investment vehicles.

What should my son do? If he goes to Florida this year, Millie will not be there. If he waits until next year, Millie will be there, but he may not have earned enough money to go. While I cannot give you advice on relationships, I will try to help you earn enough money to go to Florida, or anywhere else, when your Millie is there.

▪ WHAT WE KNOW ▪

1. Junk bonds pay high coupons because the risk of default is higher.

2. The proceeds of those high coupons can be utilized for personal or business purposes.

3. The high coupons may or may not result in future relationships.

CHAPTER 4

THE JUNK BOND MARKET

Junk bonds have been around since the beginning of the public capital markets. These junk bonds represented the primary debt of companies that had fallen on hard times.

The modern junk bond market, however, includes new initial public offerings (IPOs) and active trading. In the 1980s this market was dominated by Michael Milken at the brokerage firm Drexel Burnham. He was able to convince the investment community that many companies rated below investment grade were creditworthy enough that these companies should have access to the new issue market. His thesis was that every bond has a price it should trade at, and weaker companies could issue new bonds at higher coupons. The theory was that while some of these weaker companies would default, not all of them would and the returns of the portfolio would reward investors.

Previously, junk bonds did not represent a significant new issue market. Rather, they were investment grade bonds that fell into the junk bond category when the issuer's credit became impaired by its performance or prospects and the bonds then traded in the secondary market at discounted prices. These bonds were known as *fallen angels*. Milken's innovation involved having Drexel focus on the issuance of subordinated debt of risky companies, for which Drexel charged underwriting fees of 3% or more, which were unlike the slim spreads (prices) charged in new issues of investment grade bonds. Through these actions, Milken built a huge origination and distribution business around junk bonds.

Drexel successfully issued bonds for such companies as MGM/UA and MCI Corp., thereby building a network of believers, who then fueled the demand for subsequent IPOs (new issues) that Milken underwrote. These believers were individuals who built financial companies such as life insurance companies and savings-and-loan companies (S&Ls) around the extra coupon advantages the high yields offered. For example, an S&L would pay the federally guaranteed depositors a little more than its competitors and invest in Drexel junk bonds at several percentage points more than it paid out.

Unfortunately, Milken eventually turned his considerable powers toward supporting smaller companies' or individuals' desires to take over more established companies through what became known as *hostile takeovers*. Consequently, he orchestrated the takeover of many target companies, replacing management and placing substantial debt on the target companies' books. Junk bonds, and Drexel, were also involved with *greenmail*—in which enough shares are purchased of a public company to threaten takeover—and other nefarious financial schemes that attracted negative government interest. Oftentimes speculators—greenmailers—would buy 5% to 10% of a company's outstanding stock and then threaten to take over the company and replace management unless management bought up their stock at a profit to these greenmailers. Carl Icahn tried to buy Phillips Petroleum and walked away with millions in profits. T. Boone Pickens, Ron Perelman, and the Bass Brothers constantly engaged in takeover battles.

In 1990, there was a political backlash against hostile leveraged transactions and greenmail. As a result, junk bonds, which figured prominently in the financing of these transactions, received negative attention and scrutiny. The raiders lacked political acumen, and their responses to the criticism stoked the fires of public anger.

In response, the U.S. government mustered its full power to bring down Drexel and Milken, which caused panic in the junk bond world. The Federal Reserve prohibited banks from investing in *highly leveraged transactions* (HLTs). The savings-and-loan regulators demanded that the companies divest their junk bonds immediately without consideration of the marketplace and the consequences to the S&Ls. Consequently, not only did the S&L companies that had invested in junk bonds experience tremendous financial problems but also the entire S&L industry became destabilized, impacting the junk bond industry in return. The state insurance regulators effectively did the same to the insurance industry by steeply increasing reserve margins for holding junk bonds to a level that made their investments uneconomical.

Then the Internal Revenue Service (IRS) launched a study to do away with the interest deductibility of junk bonds. Milken went to jail; Drexel went bankrupt; and junk bond prices plummeted. Milken's life insurance and savings-and-loan junk bond clients lost their companies as their junk bond losses mounted. In addition, the closure of the market caused many companies that needed capital to go bankrupt as the banks would not lend to them.

After the fall of Milken and Drexel, the major Wall Street firms entered the junk bond market. There were no more green-mail deals, and for a long while there were no more hostile take-overs. Today's market is still centered on takeovers, but these now have the more palatable name of *private equity deals*. Iron-ically, today's list of takeover specialists is populated by many of the same individuals who sponsored the high yield takeovers of the 1990s, including former Drexel bankers who are now buy-out specialists. But while these sponsors have matured politi-cally, now making large financial contributions to politicians, their financial modus operandi is the same: they burden target companies with high debt that often requires severe cutbacks in needed capital investment, R&D, or employee reductions. Many of the companies in the last down cycle (2007 to 2008) that defaulted did so because they had too much debt and declining cash flow: the same financial engineering of the notorious late 1980s and early 1990s. The same private equity investors loaded up their acquisitions with too much debt.

SIZE, GROWTH, AND RETURNS

With more than $1 trillion in U.S. junk bonds outstanding as of March 31, 2010, the junk bond market is large. The growth of the junk bond market is tied to the economy and, impor-tantly, to the volume of private equity transactions. High yield returns generally outperformed equity returns over the past 1-, 5-, 10-, 15-, and 18½-year periods ending March 31, 2010. Obviously, different time periods show different comparisons. We are using the time period of October 1, 1991, to March 31, 2010, because this is the period during which I used the Strong-Horse Method of investing. The Appendix has the full detail of the track records. It is fair to say high yield returns are competitive with returns of most other asset classes, including stocks.

As of March 31, 2010, the average yield for investment grade bonds was 4.6%, while it was 8.4% for high yield bonds. It is important to note that *yield* does not necessarily mean *return* since many bonds default and do not provide a return. Over the past 10 years, the annualized returns for Bank of America (BoA) Merrill Lynch's high yield and investment grade indices were 7.6% and 6.7%, respectively, while the Strong-Horse investment style returned 9.4% (Table 4.1).

The high yield market is more volatile than the high grade market, but it is less volatile than the equities market, as defined by the S&P 500 Index. The S&P 500 is an index of 500 large companies with actively traded stocks and is the equity benchmark we will use for the purposes of this book. We will use the BoA Merrill Lynch High Yield Index as a proxy for high yield returns. Fundamental credit analysis is the key to success; this tends to be borne

Table 4.1 Annualized Comparable Returns October 1, 1991, Through March 31, 2010*

Return	S&P 500	BoA Merrill Lynch HY Index[†]	Strong Horse
1 yr	49.8%	57.0%	64.5%
5 yr	1.9%	7.7%	8.2%
10 yr	-0.7%	7.6%	9.4%
15 yr	7.8%	7.7%	10.3%
18½ yr	8.3%	8.7%	11.9%

*For illustrative purposes. Assume rounding at all times.

[†]The Bank of America Merrill Lynch U.S. High Yield Constrained Index (HUC0) contains all the securities in the BoA Merrill Lynch U.S. High Yield Index, but it caps issuer exposure at 2%. Index constituents are capitalization weighted, based on their current amount outstanding, provided the total allocation to an individual issuer does not exceed 2%.

Sources: BoA Merrill Lynch High Yield Bond Indices and Nomura Corporate Research and Asset Management, High Yield Total Return Institutional Composite (HYTRIC). Used by permission.

out over a long time period. Making money using fundamental credit analysis has become a profitable profession. The Strong-Horse Method is a form of fundamental credit analysis that looks for "good junk bond credits" at a cheap price.

The Strong-Horse Method is to bonds what the Benjamin Graham method is to stocks: a systematic approach to investing in the bonds of companies that have good value. This approach is also equivalent to value investing in bonds. Junk bonds are the closest to stocks in the corporate risk-reward spectrum, and they can be analyzed in a similar way. Value investing seeks to invest in companies that are undervalued by some fundamental metric—for example, companies that might have a low P/E ratio or a low price/book ratio. Using such fundamental considerations as earnings, cash flow, leverage, and financial trends, Strong-Horse Investing looks for companies whose creditworthiness is *stronger* than their bond rating. That better creditworthiness translates into expected higher price movement.

· WHAT WE KNOW ·

1. Junk bonds have been around a long time. They have been associated primarily with stressed, distressed, or failing companies.

2. The modern junk bond market has become prominent in the past 35 years.

3. The market is closely associated with new, low rated debt issuance for private equity takeover deals.

4. My fundamental Strong-Horse Investing credit evaluation approach has navigated this market successfully.

CHAPTER 5

CORPORATE BOND RATINGS AND YIELDS

One man's junk may be another man's treasure. Whether collectible items fit in one category or another will depend on several intangible factors: condition, aesthetic, and rarity. It's a little clearer cut with junk bond classification because of corporate bond ratings. Recently, however, rating agencies have come under intense criticism from many sources, including members of Congress, for their role in the collapse of the housing and mortgage markets. This criticism is related to the structured finance ratings that were applied to pools of mortgage securities. These ratings involved a more esoteric, complicated, and fundamentally flawed process than the process employed by the agencies' corporate bond ratings teams. Understanding the rating process for bonds is a critical component in analyzing high yield companies.

There are three major bond rating agencies: Moody's, Standard & Poor's (S&P), and Fitch. While the ratings between the three sometimes differ, there is a high correlation between them. For that reason, and for simplicity, we will use the S&P ratings when we discuss corporate bonds. One can make money studying the difference in each agency's rating, but we will ignore that here.

Prior to issuing debt, a company typically has that debt rated by the rating agencies. The company will provide historical and projected financial statements and present its case to the agencies to obtain the highest possible rating. The higher the rating, the lower the interest rate the company has to pay to bondholders. I have brought companies to the rating agencies in the past. When the company presents a beautiful picture, it is the job of the rating agencies to poke holes in it. Sometimes the agencies do not succeed in doing so, but often they do.

Investment grade bonds are rated AAA, AA, A, and BBB with pluses and minuses (for example, AA+ or AA−). Junk bonds are rated BB, B, or CCC, with pluses and minuses. Table 5.1 shows the ratings, yields, and spreads over the comparable maturity Treasury rates the companies had to pay to issue debt as of June 30, 2010. For example, if a 10-year Treasury is yielding 3% and a high yield corporate bond of the same maturity is yielding 10%, then the spread is 700 basis points (bp)—or 7%, since a *basis point* is 1/100 of 1%.

Figure 5.1 is a graph of the yield to maturity of different ratings as of June 30, 2010.

Table 5.1 Yields and Spreads as of June 30, 2010

S&P RATING	YTM*	SPREAD (BP)†
10-yr Treasury	2.95%	—
U.S. Corporate Master	4.33%	138
AAA	2.96%	1
AA	3.36%	41
A	4.17%	122
BBB	4.97%	202
U.S. High Yield Master	9.05%	610
BB	7.46%	451
B	8.84%	589
CCC	13.05%	1,010

*Yield to maturity (YTM) is the bond's annual return if held until maturity.

†Spread refers to the number of basis points (a basis point is 1/100 of 1%) over the comparable maturity Treasury, which in this case is the 10-year U.S. Treasury bill.

Source: BoA Merrill Lynch various bond indices as of June 30, 2010. For example, the U.S. High Yield Master and U.S. Corporate Master are series H0A0. Used by permission.

Figure 5.1 Yield to Maturity Comparison as of June 30, 2010*

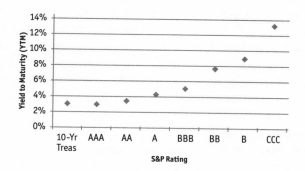

*For illustrative purposes. Assume rounding at all times.

Source: BoA Merrill Lynch various bond indices as of June 30, 2010. Used by permission.

SPREADS VERSUS PRICES

Bond professionals talk in terms of spreads, not prices. *Spread* refers to the number of basis points (1/100 of 1%) over the comparable maturity Treasury. (You will see later in this chapter that bond prices and bond yields are mathematically convertible from one to the other.) The risk is implied in the spread, whereas it is not implied in the price. Generally, a 450 bp spread in Table 5.1 implied a BB credit, while a 600 bp spread implied a B credit in June 2010.

Rating agencies employ a serious group of trained professionals who are proficient at analyzing corporate bond risk. Nevertheless, they have some limitations that have spawned a generation of professional credit analysts. When assessing a company's bond rating, agencies do not factor in the price of an underlying bond, only the company's financial data. While they may question management as to the future, they do not fully penalize management for the expected results—they are reactive, not proactive. It is not that they cannot project the future. Rather, when they lowered ratings in the past based on expected future performance, the investment community complained that they were hurting them by downgrading companies too frequently. Over the years, the ratings agencies have developed communications tools to point out their views on expected outlooks.

One must consider the importance of the relationship between corporate bond ratings and corporate yields. When a company issues debt in the bond market, its rating is a key factor in the interest rate it will pay as long as the bonds remain outstanding. Thus, it is crucial that a company issuing debt presents itself in the best possible light.

Let's go back to our old friend Millie. She has since graduated from college, and she has grown her small business into a major messenger company in her hometown of Denver, Colorado. In addition to her original bike services, she has added car and truck services. Unfortunately, business isn't as easy as it once was. Millie is facing fierce competition from Billy's Messengering, LLC. Prices have become competitive, profit margins are slim, and demand is split between the two competitors. Millie knows that in this economic landscape her business is not sustainable. After much thought, she ultimately decides that she must buy out Billy's company in order to have sustainable future growth. However, since she does not have the cash on hand to simply buy him out, she must—once again—add debt in what is known as a *leveraged buyout* (LBO). To pursue her plan, Millie will need to approach the rating agencies with certain financial data about her company's assets and operations.

A common metric (but not the only metric) used in corporate valuation is *earnings **before** interest, taxes, depreciation, and **a**mortization* (EBITDA), which can be calculated by subtracting cash costs from revenue (explained further in the Appendix). We will use EBITDA as a metric for cash flow and for profit, even though it is not a perfect measure because it excludes capital expenditures. Companies need to spend capital to maintain, modernize, and grow their business. EBITDA is not a generally accepted accounting measure, but analysts use it all the time. When you use it, make sure that the company has adequate cash flow for maintenance and modernization.

Millie's once-small business is now making *revenues* of $25 million per year. However, she has *costs* too, lots of them. In the past year she spent $15 million on salaries; maintaining her expensive fleet of cars, trucks, and bikes; cartons; and other items necessary to run a messenger service. She also had *selling, general, and administrative* (SG&A) *expenses*, which included marketing costs to advertise in the local newspaper and paying marketing salaries. Millie paid $5 million in SG&A expenses in the past year. Millie also paid $5 million in depreciation *expenses* on her fleet of vehicles. *Depreciation* is a noncash charge that spreads out the cost of a tangible asset over its useful life. Millie paid no *interest expenses* because she has not yet taken any debt. All these figures, of course, can be consolidated into the single table of an income statement.

Millie is now contemplating taking on debt, thereby *leveraging* her company—a word with a negative connotation after the recent financial crisis. One commonly used measure of *leverage* is the amount of debt incurred by a company in relation to its ability to fund that debt out of its current operations. That measure we call *debt to EBITDA*. Millie's Messengering's EBITDA is $5 million ($25 million revenue − $15 million costs − $5 million SG&A expenses = $5 million).

In Tables 5.2 and 5.3, we can take a look at Millie's and Billy's income statements (in millions of dollars). Millie's costs are just as high as her revenues: she is breaking even. Currently, Billy has the same problem. But Millie believes that if she buys out Billy's Messengering, she can acquire Billy's revenue with only marginal increases to her costs. By combining their operations, Millie will achieve certain economies of scale that will ultimately make the combined companies profitable. With the infrastructure already in place to run a messengering business, Millie's combined business will experience significant cost savings while maintaining (and eventually expanding) operations. For example, Millie will not need two dispatchers or two advertising departments. If her calculations are correct, Millie will be able to turn a profit in the next year.

Table 5.2
Millie's Messengering Income Statement (in Millions of Dollars)

MILLIE'S MESSENGERING	
Revenue	25
Costs	15
SG&A	5
Depreciation	5
Interest	0
Pretax	0
Tax	0
Net income	0
EBITDA	5

Table 5.3
Billy's Messengering Income Statement (in Millions of Dollars)

BILLY'S MESSENGERING	
Revenue	20
Costs	12
SG&A	4
Depreciation	4
Interest	0
Pretax	0
Tax	0
Net income	0
EBITDA	4

Millie approaches Billy with an offer to buy his business. She points out that they are harming each other and that the two competitors are not sustainable. She shows him comparable purchase prices of six times the EBITDA in other cities for messenger service companies. Billy immediately accepts, thinking that anyone willing to pay him $24 million for a company with zero net income is crazy. Now Millie needs the financing to complete the purchase. The outcome may vary depending on certain assumptions made by the rating agencies, as described below and in Tables 5.4 and 5.5.

Best Case

The banks are unwilling to lend the $24 million, but the ABC Securities Company junk bond department thinks that it can sell junk bonds to mutual funds and pension funds provided that Millie gets her fledging company's debt rated. ABC takes her to the rating agencies and explains that Millie can cut operating costs by $4 million and selling costs (SG&A) by $1 million for a $5 million savings. Under these circumstances, Millie's EBITDA would be her $5 million + Billy's $4 million + $5 million in savings for a total of $14 million. She can pay the debt off in less than 2 years. $24 million of debt and $14 million of EBITDA. Millie is rated CCC+ and will pay a 9% interest rate, resulting in $2.2 million in annual interest payments.

Agency Rating: CCC+

Worst Case

The rating agencies refuse to accept Millie's costs savings estimates and assume instead that there are no cost savings. Furthermore, the rating services say revenue could fall by $5 million as Billy's clients go elsewhere, and it could take 6 years to pay off $24 million of debt and $4 million of EBITDA. They assign Millie a CCC rating. In today's market that could imply an 11% yield or $2.6 million per year in interest.

Agency Rating: CCC

Table 5.4
Millie's Messengering's Best Case (in Millions of Dollars)

Revenue	45
Costs	23
SG&A	8
Depreciation	9
Interest	2.2
Pretax	2.8
Tax	1.4
Net income	1.4
EBITDA	14

Table 5.5
Millie's Messengering's Worst Case (in Millions of Dollars)

Revenue	40
Costs	27
SG&A	9
Depreciation	9
Interest	2.6
Pretax	-7.6
Tax	—
Net i ncome	-7.6
EBITDA	4

Best Case

This scenario yields Millie a debt-to-EBITDA ratio of 24:14 or 1.7 times, a healthy rate.

Worst Case

However, the worst-case scenario gives her a debt-to-EBITDA ratio of 24:4 or 6:1 and interest coverage of less than 2.0. These numbers are poor for a small company with no track record as a combined entity.

Whether or not Millie's acquisition makes sense at all, we'll get to in Chapter 6 on credit analysis.

· WHAT WE KNOW ·

1. The rating agencies are an important component of the debt capital markets.

2. The ratings of the three agencies—Moody's, Standard & Poor's, and Fitch—are highly correlated.

3. The assigned rating often determines the offering price or yield that a new issuance will pay.

4. The rating professionals are good corporate credit analysts.

5. A common measure of cash flow is earnings before interest, taxes, depreciation, and amortization (EBITDA).

6. A common measure of price is the basis point spread over the same maturity Treasury.

7. Millie is either one brave girl or foolhardy, depending on what credit analysis shows.

8. Millie's use of massive amounts of debt shows that she can very easily become a private equity entrepreneur.

CHAPTER 6

CREDIT ANALYSIS: HOW DO YOU KNOW WHEN A COMPANY HAS TOO MUCH DEBT?

What do Dumbledore and Gandalf have in common with credit analysis? Actually, you may be asking, who are Dumbledore and Gandalf?

Both are wizards in movies (and originally books): Dumbledore in *Harry Potter* and Gandalf in *The Lord of the Rings* trilogy. They are master strategists who analyze all the information available to them, work to get needed current information, and forecast the future. I am not saying you need to be a wizard to perform credit analysis, but it would not hurt. Credit analysis means knowing everything about a company—understanding the past, searching the present, and anticipating the future.

Wizards can do almost anything, and that's one of the reasons movies about wizards are so great. My children introduced me to Dumbledore and Gandalf years ago, first in the books and then the movies; I was immediately hooked on them. But wizards as credit analysts? Admittedly, the idea is a little far-fetched (they are too busy saving the world). So we will have to leave credit analysis to us mere mortals. Nevertheless, there *is* a similarity between what wizards do and what credit analysts do.

We actually started a credit analysis when Millie bought Billy's messenger service. In the worst case, the leverage for the acquisition defined as total debt divided by EBITDA rose from zero (no debt) to 6:1. This meant it would take Millie six years to pay down her debt given the expected worst-case earnings. Furthermore, she barely had enough cash to make her interest payment (and scarce capital for reinvestment).

Credit analysis is not hard to do, but it requires attention to detail. Most times you cannot detect fraud, but sometimes you can. The starting point is a company's financial statement. Public companies must report their financials to the SEC, and you can access their filings on the government website (www.sec.gov). It is a different story for private companies. You would be surprised at how many companies do not want to release these statements.

Let's assume you now have the financials. Check trends. Look at the size and growth of the earnings and cash flow. How is the business doing? Read what management is saying about its performance. Are there any new developments that you should know about? Has the company added any significant debt? Why? What project is the company spending on?

I like to look further into the key risk factors section when researching a company. Sometimes it is significant litigation, or sometimes new competitors or new technologies render the company's main products obsolete. I also like to see what conflicts of interest senior management has. Compensation is a key factor. I like to see a management team have the same incentives as investors. However, this process is tricky. When management has a vested interest as shareholders, they can abuse this privilege and work to seize value from bondholders for their own best interest. Management's vested interests are congruent with the interests of other shareholders; their interests are not congruent with the interests of bondholders.

THE THREE TYPES OF RISK

Corporate credit analysis is the assessment of the ability of a company to borrow and repay its debt obligations. It is similar to equity security analysis with one big difference: it focuses on debt. I'll turn to credit analysis later, but let's take a look at a framework in which to think about credit risk. There are three main risks to consider: *business, financial,* and *covenant.* All are important, but some are more important than others.

1. Business Risk

Business risk is the core risk, and its analysis is most similar to equity analysis: it is the assessment of the quality of a company's operations. Can the company earn enough over a long time period to survive and grow in its marketplace? Start with the company's revenue and earnings growth. Look at the company's cost structure. Perform a multiyear margin analysis: gross margin, operating margin, and EBITDA margin. Are there signs of increasing cost pressure? Look at its market share, and compare that to its competitors'. Are there any troubling signs?

If a company cannot run its business profitably, it should not have access to capital. A company has to have a sustainable core capability, or it should not exist. It should be able to sustain itself and grow over the investment horizon. All companies run into trouble at some time, but as investors, we should have confidence that the company can right itself. Below are examples of how a company can fail by having high business risk.

Product Obsolescence (an Example of Too Much Business Risk)

Technology has changed the way certain industries work. For example, few people look up telephone numbers using a yellow pages directory anymore. On top of that, the phone companies added a financial cost to access telephone numbers through operators. Google made yellow pages almost obsolete by enabling people to look up phone numbers for free. The directory companies that specialized in publishing phone numbers and selling advertising all went bankrupt quickly as their earnings nose-dived.

The publishing industry itself has been hurt by the proliferation of information on the web. Once-proud news companies, such as *Newsweek* and *BusinessWeek*, have had to be sold to survive. Newspapers have folded for the same reasons. Advertising dollars have remained about the same but are now spread out over many additional players, hurting the profitability of traditional sources. Similarly, radio and broadcast television have all been severely hurt. Here's an example.

Dex One (formerly R.H. Donnelley) is the third largest yellow pages provider (publishing and advertising of local telephone numbers in a printed book) in the United States, behind AT&T and SuperMedia (formerly Idearc, which was spun off by Verizon and subsequently went bankrupt in March 2009).

In the years leading up to its June 2009 bankruptcy, R.H. Donnelley faced rapidly declining advertising sales, the lifeblood of its dying industry. We don't normally look at net income, but the numbers are impressive enough to mention. Between 2008 and 2009: $8.75 billion in losses! Nearly $10 billion in debt! Declining sales of 20%! As you can see in Table 6.1, advertising sales dropped from $2.7 billion to $2.0 billion in two years.

Table 6.1 Dex One Corporation's Sales Versus Debt (in Billions of Dollars)

	ADVERTISING SALES	CHANGE	TOTAL DEBT
2007	$2,745.7	—	$10,175.7
2008	$2,547.7	−7.2%	$9,622.3
2009	$2,028.7	−20.4%	$3,554.8
Source: The figures for Dex One are from its 10-K Form, which is available through www.sec.gov.			

R.H. Donnelley was a victim of obsolescence, but ultimately it failed because of its overleverage. It also had a high cost structure due to its relatively high cost of selling ads through a sales force. After filing for Chapter 11 bankruptcy in May 2009 and shedding $6.4 *billion* of debt obligations, Dex One was reborn on February 1, 2010, when it began trading on the New York Stock Exchange (NYSE). However, even after the company was reborn, Dex One failed to mitigate the fundamental business risk at the core of its operations. As a result, the stock dropped steadily from $35.00 on February 2 to $8.50, as of October 2010. The company has shifted its strategy to electronic media, but it does not have the same market share as it did before electronic competition.

Declining Earnings

Declining EBITDA, operating earnings, and any other earnings measures that a company reports are another type of business risk that a company may face. Simply put, if a company's revenue is not greater than its cost of goods sold and SG&A expenses, it is at risk of failure. General Motors (GM) provides a good example here.

Meeting fierce competition from Japanese manufacturers Honda and Toyota, GM's sales declines snowballed as the company lost significant market share in the market it had once dominated. Table 6.2 shows the change of General Motors' domestic sales from 1998 to 2009.

Table 6.2 General Motors' U.S. Automobile Sales

CALENDAR YEAR	TOTAL U.S. SALES (UNITS)	CHG/YR
1998	4,603,991	–
1999	5,017,150	+9.0%
2000	4,953,163	−1.3%
2001	4,904,015	−1.0%
2002	4,858,705	−0.9%
2003	4,756,403	−2.1%
2004	4,707,416	−1.0%
2005	4,517,730	−4.0%
2006	4,124,645	−8.7%
2007	3,866,620	−6.3%
2008	2,980,688	−22.9%
2009	2,084,492	−30.1%

In addition to declining sales, General Motors took heavy losses of $10.8 billion in 2008, the year leading up to its June 1, 2009, bankruptcy filing (Table 6.3). In bankruptcy, the U.S. government forced bondholders to replace $27 billion of debt for only 10% of the equity of the new company, with an option to buy more. As you can see in Table 6.3, General Motors' declining car sales, resulting poor revenue trends, and operating losses are examples of high business risk, which in the case of General Motors, resulted in its inability to support its debt load.

Table 6.3 General Motors' Financials (in Billions of Dollars)

	REVENUE	OPERATING EARNINGS*
2006	$204,467.0	$5,262.0
2007	$179,984.0	$212.0
2008	$148,979.0	−$10,761.0
*Operating earnings = gross profit − SG&A.		

Mergers and Acquisitions

Merger and acquisition transactions fail when the combined companies do not work together smoothly. Expected costs savings may not be achieved, or expected revenue additions may not come about. For example, in the Millie-Billy merger, many of Billy's clients may not want to use Millie's service. The resultant financial condition could mean precarious and unsustainable debt levels.

2. Financial Risk

Financial risk is the risk that a company takes when it takes on more debt than is prudent. Just as homeowners should not take on too large a mortgage lest they suffer the consequence of losing their homes, so too should companies not overborrow and risk losing their assets. The junk bond landscape is littered with bankrupt companies that were once quite successful but, for reasons only known to the CEO and a select few, overborrowed.

Paradoxically, the companies with the best operations often can borrow the most and have the worst balance sheets. Lenders frequently limit the amount of debt companies with high business risk can borrow. When considering a bond purchase, it is not enough to simply look at a leverage ratio and make a determination of whether you will lend to a company. One must understand the leverage risk in the context of business risk. When recruiting new college graduates to join my firm, I would often hand the candidates financial statistics of two companies in the same industry: one for a more highly leveraged growing retailer and one that had low leverage but five years of declining sales and profitability. I would ask the candidates to pick the better credit risk and explain their answer (the declining company with lower leverage subsequently went bankrupt).

I can categorize overborrowing in two ways: *business plan borrowing* and *private equity* (PE) *transactions.*

Business Plan Borrowing

Business plan borrowing takes place when there are no revenues. This type of borrowing worked for the cable TV industry, which was initially a dream of some entrepreneurs. Favorable legislation and regulation allowed the cable companies to borrow and then string cable to customers' homes. The product was successful and desirable, and the entrepreneurs priced their products successfully. Major companies such as Comcast and Cablevision were created this way. Unfortunately, this method did not work for other technology build-outs, such as various telephone businesses that failed in the 2000 to 2001 period, which consequently triggered the 2001 recession.

Some of these failed businesses included two global satellite companies (Iridium and Globalstar), a company that strung cable under the Atlantic Ocean for cheap transatlantic commu-nication (Global Crossing), and several companies that tried to deliver high-speed Internet capability to the home. All of these companies borrowed heavily up front and were not able to gen-erate enough revenue to meet their debt reduction assumptions in their business plans.

Private Equity Transactions

When a private equity firm acquires a company, it will often use a significant amount of debt to finance the transaction. A com-mon practice is to place this debt on the balance sheet of the acquired company and use cash flow from the newly acquired company to pay down this additional debt. Sometimes a private equity firm will turn around an acquired company by providing capital injections and better management. But the debt used in the acquisition creates a substantial risk, leverages the com-pany to the limit, and reduces its creditworthiness. Legacy bond issues not protected by covenants often decline substantially.

Private equity transactions place too much debt on other-wise good companies. Most acquisitions are leveraged to the greatest possible level. The amount of leverage allowed is based on the amount of debt lenders are willing to provide. During takeover battles between private equity combatants, the parties fight over who can pay shareholders the most. They often pay so much that they load too much debt on the company's books. The result is that the taken-over company has no room to make a mistake or withstand a downturn.

These types of transactions are good for Wall Street. The mergers and acquisitions (M&A) departments collect an M&A fee (typically 1% of the value of the transaction). There is usually an investment banking fee. The private equity firms typically take various banking fees. The securities firms take a fee (sometimes as high as 3%) for issuing and distributing junk bond debt, and the commercial banks get a fee for lending to the deal. Lawyers and accountants get large fees as these deals are legal and accounting intensive.

A private equity deal could not happen without both the bank debt and junk bonds. Assume the following:

Value of assets = liabilities + value of equity
Value of equity = value of assets – liabilities

If the value of assets stays constant, each dollar of debt reduction increases the value of the equity. The implications of this scenario are that private equity financiers place as much debt (liability) on the books of a company as they believe it could possibly withstand, and then they work to reduce that debt as quickly as possible. During the hostile takeover years, they put so much debt on the books that cash flow could not cover the interest expense in year 1. They overcame this obstacle by issuing *zero coupon bonds*, or *payment-in-kind bonds*, meaning that the interest did not have to be paid in cash in the early years. The debt, instead, kept increasing with each interest payment. The hope was that the growth of cash flow would exceed the growth of debt. Unfortunately, this often did not happen. Default rates those years rose to 7.2% in 1989, 10.9% in 1990, and 11.5% in 1991. The recent 2008 bubble resulted in a 10.3% default rate.

Again, for every dollar of debt reduction, equity increases by a dollar. So private equity companies fund the acquired companies with mountains of debt and work to reduce that debt by various means, such as firing employees, slashing research and development budgets, and reducing capital expenditures. They operate the business for short-term gains at the expense of long-term value. Certainly, if the owners see a growth opportunity to enhance value over time, they will seize it, but, in my experience, this long-term view is the exception.

I have actually understated the value of the equity above. If we assume a company can be sold for eight times its EBITDA, then every dollar of increased cash flow can increase the value of the company, and thus the value of the equity can be increased by $8. While this move is shortsighted, many private equity investors run their businesses for the short run. In the long run, however, as more and more public companies get swallowed up by private equity, the lack of investment is not good for the economy or the country.

A typical capital structuring in a private equity deal would look as follows:

Typical Private Equity Capitalization

Bank Debt	50%
High Yield Debt	25%
Equity	25%
	100%

Debt here is three times equity, or 75% of the capitalization. While this figure is important in the event of a bankruptcy, most professionals look to the amount of debt relative to the ability to generate cash flow:

Debt/Cash Flow   or   Debt/EBITDA

They also look at interest coverage. Generally, debt of six times EBITDA or interest of two times EBITDA can be financed.

These ratios vary depending on the economy and the "feeling" in the market; they also vary with the costs of debt. For example, just before the 2007 meltdown, when spreads were tight (approaching 200 basis points), the interest cost was so low that debt levels rose to eight or ten times cash flow. When financing costs rose, many of these companies ran into financial difficulty.

"Typical" is loosely defined here, and the amount and type of debt and equity can shift dramatically. When the market is buoyant and lenders are throwing money at deals, the equity could be significantly less than 25%. Teams of financial engineers are constantly tinkering with the "ideal cap structure." Some innovations include *second lien debt*, which would increase the amount of secured debt above the junk bonds in the priority of payment.

Other "innovations" are designed to reduce the equity component, increase the leverage, and provide higher returns to the equity sponsors. Unfortunately, the higher debt burden reduces the creditworthiness of the acquired company and increases the probability of failure. Many once-proud companies have failed because of these transactions. Here are three examples of *failed private equity transactions*:

1. The Simmons Bedding Company is a manufacturer of mattresses in the United States. In November 2003, T.H. Lee Partners agreed to acquire Simmons. In September 2009, Simmons filed for Chapter 11.

2. Aleris International is a manufacturer of aluminum products with headquarters in Beachwood, Ohio. In December

2006, the Texas Pacific Group completed its acquisition of Aleris for approximately $1.6 billion. Aleris filed for Chapter 11 in February 2009.

3. The Tribune Company, the Chicago-based multimedia corporation, is the owner of such notable newspapers as the *Chicago Tribune* and the *Los Angeles Times*, television network WGN America, and the Chicago Cubs baseball team. In 2007, real estate entrepreneur Samuel Zell acquired Tribune, and the company subsequently filed for Chapter 11 bankruptcy in December 2008.

Financial risk is the risk that an otherwise good business could fail because it takes on too much debt. That debt obligation may force the company to operate in a matter that is harmful to creditors.

3. Covenant Risk

You now own the bonds of a great company: good products, improving profitability, and not too much debt. What can go wrong? Plenty. For example, the business could deteriorate, or the management team could engage in some dishonest activity. You could also have the company's creditworthiness reduced by the very people you entrusted to run the business. How can that happen? They could pay themselves a high dividend; or they could spin off the best assets to shareholders. There are a number of other things they could do. This reduction can be mitigated with adequate covenants in the bond indenture. This concept is so important that I devote all of Chapter 17 to it later in the book.

• WHAT WE KNOW •

1. Credit analysis is the basic building block of junk bond investing.

2. To start a credit analysis, you must access a company's financials. One place to do this is the government website www.sec.gov. There are numerous other sites on which to access this information for a fee such as a Bloomberg terminal. Also, you can access financials on a company's own website.[1]

3. The three key components of credit analysis discussed in this chapter are:

   - *Business risk.* Check the strength of a company's operations. Pay particular attention to the earnings and cash flow trends.

   - *Financial risk.* Look at the company's debt level in relation to its cash flow.

   - *Covenant risk.* This will be discussed further in Chapter 17.

4. Private equity transactions typically reduce a target's creditworthiness by placing a tower of debt on otherwise good companies.

5. Millie's business in combination with Billy's introduces increased business risk and financial risk. The key consideration is that the new company is very small with only a short track record. This business risk trumps the worst-case scenario financial risk, which is only modestly adequate. On balance, I would wait for the new company to mature.

CHAPTER 7

THE STRONG-HORSE METHOD

If you are a wizard and interested in credit analysis, you might not need this chapter. Mere mortals, however, need a structure for investing in the bonds of risky companies. I will now discuss my structure, Strong-Horse Investing, in greater detail with important benchmarks to aid you in making decisions. As mentioned, the image of a "strong horse" describes what we are looking for: power and speed.

The Strong-Horse Method is a two-step approach. The first step is to conduct the fundamental credit analysis. A Strong-Horse company is one that can improve in creditworthiness and generate excess cash flow to pay down debt over time. Such a company is a market share leader, a low cost producer, and in control of its future. It generates excess cash flow to pay off its debt obligations. Below is a list of some Strong-Horse characteristics:

1. Market share leader

2. Low cost producer

3. Product pricing leader

4. Solid management team

5. Improving product trends

6. Generating excess cash flow

7. Controllable debt levels

8. History of paying down debt

9. Good covenants

All of the above credit characteristics seem obvious, but it is rare that you see a junk bond issuer with *all* of them. These characteristics are ideals. Therefore, we have to perform a credit analysis and calibrate where in the credit continuum each company is located. To do that there are financial analytical principles I use to supplement the credit characteristics. These principles are explained in the sidebar "Five Principles of Strong-Horse Financial Credit Analysis."

THE FIVE PRINCIPLES OF STRONG-HORSE FINANCIAL CREDIT ANALYSIS

The five important principles that you must adhere to for Strong-Horse Investing to work for you are described below.

Principle 1. It Is Better If the Company You Invest in Has More Cash Flow Than Less Cash Flow

Companies that generate significant excess free cash flow must be doing something right. They may have a good product with pricing flexibility, or their costs are under control. These companies can withstand a sudden downturn, they can spend to fend off competition, or they can acquire a needed product line with their excess cash.

As discussed, we use EBITDA (earnings before interest, taxes, depreciation, and amortization) as a measure of cash flow, even though it is not truly cash flow. There are many noncash transactions that do not show up in the EBITDA calculation, but it is the generally accepted measure, and it is pretty good. In some respects, it is a proxy for earnings. We use this measure as it allows us to look at companies with different debt levels and tax rates. It is not perfect, but it is acceptable. The Appendix illustrates two methods of calculating EBITDA.

Principle 2. It Is Better If the Trend of Cash Flow Is Positive Rather Than Negative

Companies change over time. We want to invest in those that change in a positive way. We do not want to invest in companies whose business is on the decline. (There are specialists known as vulture or distressed debt investors, however, who invest only in failing companies and make a good living doing so. That type of investing often involves litigation, proxy fights, and fierce inter-creditor battles. In this book, we stick to looking at companies that are not bankrupt.)

We saw the yellow pages business example of a declining company in Chapter 6. Your first line of investment defense is the trend of the company. When analyzing a stock, even a decline in the growth rate of a company can cause a stock price to plummet. We are looking at a positive or negative trend in the level of EBITDA; a negative trend is a cause for concern.

Principle 3. It Is Better If Cash Flow Can Easily Pay the Company's Interest Obligations Than Not Be Able to Pay Them

A company's not being able to pay its interest obligations is an event of default. The interest coverage ratio (EBITDA/interest expense) tells us how much "cash flow" the company generates relative to the interest on its debt—how many times it can "cover" its interest payments. We want substantial financial flexibility (excess coverage) in the event of an unforeseen problem. Again, a negative trend in this ratio is a cause for concern.

Principle 4. Less Leverage Is Better Than More Leverage from a Credit Perspective

Leverage is a double-edged sword—it can bolster earnings, or it can kill earnings. We measure leverage by looking at a company's debt level in relation to the cash flow it generates to pay down debt. For purposes of this book, we will use EBITDA as the measure of cash flow. The debt leverage ratio is debt divided by EBITDA. One way of thinking about this concept is that it tells us how long it would take a company to pay off its debt using the current year's earnings. Too much debt can destroy a company, or at least hamper its ability to reinvest in the business. With cash tight, capital expenditures are often curtailed, research and development is delayed, employees are fired, and, finally, better capitalized competitors emerge to take the business away.

Principle 5. Prudently Financed Capital Expenditures (CapEx) Are Needed to Survive and Grow

Companies have to invest for the future. For companies to grow, they must get more out of their existing assets or add new assets profitably. Existing assets need maintenance capital expenditures, which can be quite expensive. Trucking companies, for example, have to replace engines or brakes fairly frequently. Blast furnaces have to be relined periodically. You should not invest in any company that cuts back on maintenance or growth expenditures. These companies are cutting back on their future, implying that their business model no longer works. Or else they have been taken over by private equity investors who have bought the company only for the purpose of making a quick flip sale to an unsuspecting investor.

These expenditures have to be paid for in a responsible manner. Maintenance capital expenditures (maintenance CapEx) should be funded out of cash flow (oftentimes management will disclose maintenance CapEx). Calculate EBITDA less maintenance CapEx; this number should be strongly positive. Capital expenditures for expansion or investment could be funded with debt, as long as the total debt level does not become burdensome. If a major project such as a new factory will be around for many years, it is reasonable for a company to borrow to fund that factory. Paying down the debt over time is equivalent to matching the asset with the funding, assuming that the return on investment (ROI) of the project is greater than the cost of capital funding the project.

The second step to the approach is to relate the results of the Strong-Horse credit analysis to the yield of the bond (Figure 7.1). Ideally, this is how it would work (here is where the rating agencies come into play): We first calibrate a credit the Strong-Horse way, and we determine that it is equivalent to a single B going to BB. Standard & Poor's correctly gives it a B rating, and it is priced like a B-rated credit. We would most likely buy it because it should appreciate in price as it gets upgraded to BB.

Figure 7.1 Relationship Between Credit and Yield
(Values as of June 30, 2010)

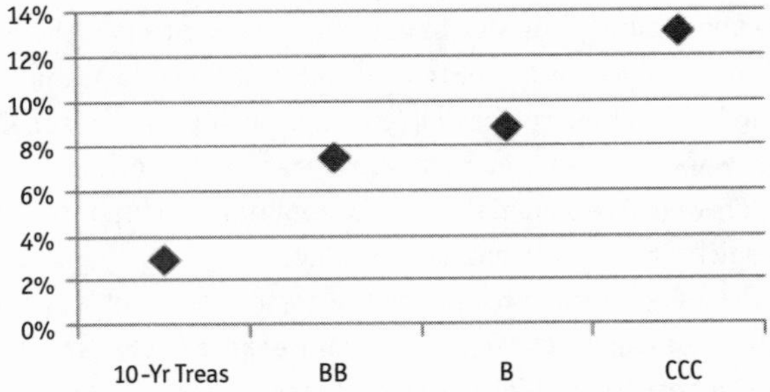

Source: BoA Merrill Lynch various bond indices as of June 30, 2010. Used by permission.

Figure 7.2 shows the relationship between credit rating and yield: spotting an underrated credit can yield additional coupon while the price simultaneously increases. Once creditworthiness is determined, look at spreads over the equivalent Treasuries. If the bond has a 9% coupon and goes up four points in one year, that is a 13% return. When the risk-free rate is zero, as it was in 2011, that is a great return.

Again looking at Figure 7.2, assume we have conducted a fundamental analysis on our junk bond, and we believe that over time the bond will be recognized as a higher-quality BB-rated bond as opposed to a B-rated bond, which is its current rating. This recognition of higher quality translates to a 2% extra yield over the life of the bond. That is, we are getting 2% extra yield on a par bond. Par equals $1,000 per bond, and convention has it written as $100. We are getting a 10% yield for a bond that should be yielding 8%. According to bond mathematics, which will be explained later, this bond is worth $1,135.90,

Figure 7.2 Hypothetical Yield Comparison

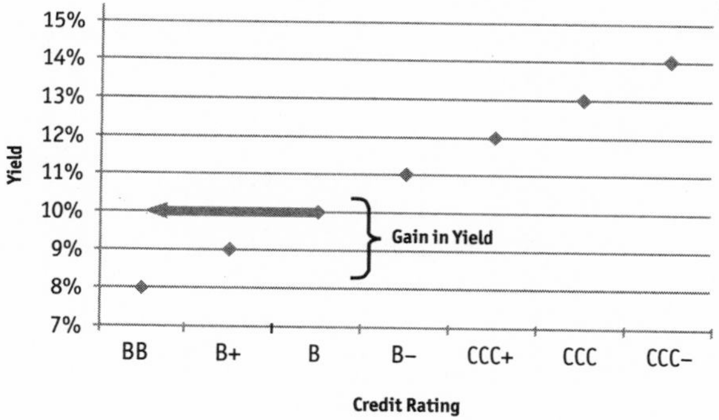

Source: BoA Merrill Lynch High Yield Bond Indices. Used by permission.

which is $135.90 more than you paid for it. The extra price makes it a Strong-Horse investment.

We want to invest money in—that is, lend to—junk bond companies because of the extra yield they offer. The beauty of compound interest is that a 3% or 6% advantage compounded over a lifetime generates substantial extra return. So $10,000 invested at 10% for 10 years is worth nearly $26,000, while the same amount invested at 4% is worth only $14,800. There is 75% more return generated by investing at a 6% advantage over 10 years. Imagine how favorable this is for a huge pension plan, compounding for 20 or 25 years.

Unfortunately, we cannot count on always receiving the extra yield. Higher yield means higher risk, and in the case of junk bonds, higher expected default rates. *You will not receive the expected return if the company you invest in defaults*. The primary reason the Strong-Horse Method returns were higher than the market returns was the ability to minimize defaults through our credit analysis. Some junk bond–issuing companies will default: companies change over time, and sometimes they fail. That is why you want to invest in companies that have a better chance of succeeding.

RULES OF THUMB

In general, any systematic approach to investment analyses has limitations, though over the years, I have seen many approaches provide excellent returns. I used a systematic approach successfully with investment grade bonds in an inflationary environment in the 1970s and early 1980s. Investor Joel Greenblatt has successfully done so with stocks, as he discusses in his book *The Magic Formula*. For purposes of this book, I will give you some benchmarks for determining credit quality, but they are just a starting point. During some cycles, they may appear too conservative. Remember, companies change over time, and you want the trend of financial performance to be your friend. Constantly update your analysis once you have committed capital. If possible, try to project the future performance of the company. You can be assisted by websites that provide analysts' earnings estimates. If independent analysts think a company's future is declining, that is not a good sign.

Table 7.1 provides Strong-Horse Benchmarks for leverage and interest coverage by Standard & Poor's rating. For example, a multi-billion-dollar company whose debt is less than 3.5 times EBITDA could be a BB candidate. However, if the trend is negative, I would be concerned. A multiyear negative trend implies the company could be in serious trouble and should be avoided. The trend comment is true for single B- and CCC-rated companies as well. Sometimes companies turn their operations

Table 7.1 Strong-Horse Benchmarks

RATING	LEVERAGE (NO GREATER THAN)	COVERAGE (NO LESS THAN)	NOTES
BB	3.5x	3.5x	Should be a very large company
B	4.5x	2.5x	Should be free cash flow positive, and not fully levered
CCC	6x	2x	Typically fully levered with no cushion

around through business and financial engineering. However, this is not always possible in a competitive world, and companies that are already weak can easily fail.

Calculate leverage and coverage. For example, let us return to Millie in Chapter 5 under the rating agency worst-case scenario. Her EBITDA could fall to $4 million; her debt could rise to $24 million and interest expense of $2.6 million per year. The debt to EBITDA would equal 6, and the EBITDA to interest of 2.6 would equal 1.50. Looking at Table 7.1, her numbers place her in the CCC range. However, as her new company is small and without much of a track record, I would discount that further.

In bond investing, one bad investment that defaults could drop 50 points and result in a loss five times greater than a huge 10-point success. One bad investment could equal five good investments; thus you want to minimize the error of an investment failure (I call these errors Type I errors). It is okay to miss good investments (I call these Type II errors) if none of your investments default.

Note that all of the above depends on your being able to calculate EBITDA. However, companies often obfuscate their presentation of it. You should focus on what is continuing cash flow in future years. If a one-time noncash transaction increases EBITDA, do not include it in your analysis.

Some Caveats

1. The rating agencies often penalize companies in certain industries or companies that emerge from bankruptcy. For example, at the time of this writing, one auto parts company, Dana Holding Corporation, is rated a low single B by one of the agencies and BB by another. As of September 2010, its statistics are closer to a BB, and its trading range is closer to a BB.

2. Many analysts give credit to the cash a company has on hand. They subtract the cash from debt if it is unencumbered. For example, Dana Holding Corporation as of September 2010 had more cash than debt.

3. While all of the above seems complex, once you have done this analysis a few times, you will realize that it is not complicated.

Remember, these are only rules of thumb; ratios are tricky, and a strong leverage ratio in one industry may be average or weak in another. For example, a trucking company's EBITDA measure could be misleading. While its cost of goods sold (COGS) may not be high, its capital expenditures (CapEx) for its trucks and their brakes that are replaced frequently at an enormous cost should really be considered part of COGS. Some analysts look at unlevered free cash flow, which is EBITDA minus CapEx.

· WHAT WE KNOW ·

1. You can make money using this credit analysis method.

2. Characteristics of a Strong-Horse company:

   - Market share leader

   - Low cost producer

   - Product pricing leader

   - Solid management team

   - Improving product trends

   - Generating excess cash flow

   - Controllable debt levels

   - History of paying down debt

   - Good covenants

3. Credit analysis is the calibration of the strength of a company's ability to repay debt.

4. Calculate creditworthiness and determine your assessed rating. Look at trends, leverage, coverage, size, and CapEx.

5. Remember the five principles of Strong-Horse financial credit analysis:

   - It is better if the company you invest in has more cash flow than less cash flow.

   - It is better if the trend of cash flow is positive rather than negative.

- It is better if cash flow can easily pay the company's interest obligations than not be able to pay them.

- Less leverage is better than more leverage from a credit perspective.

- Prudently financed capital expenditures (CapEx) are needed to survive and grow.

6. You have studied the past, understand the present, and are making a decision about the future. Our wizards would be proud of you.

CHAPTER 8

RELATING CREDIT TO PRICE

W e have now learned how to calibrate a credit. The yield you receive should compensate you for the risk you are taking. You may not get the highest yield, but it should be good enough. Sometimes the expected return is not high enough to take the investment risk.

The art of the investment comes from assessing the investment merits given the results of your Strong-Horse credit analysis. Table 8.1 shows the yield to maturity (YTM) and option-adjusted spread (OAS) ranges of the Merrill Lynch High Yield Index by rating since December 31, 2003. The range is enormous, and it takes into account the credit cycles and various crises during this time period, excluding the Lehman Brothers bankruptcy and the 2007 to 2008 credit crash.

Table 8.1 High Yield Index Option-Adjusted Spreads

	YTM	OAS (BP)
BB	6–8%	200–470
B	7–9%	287–602
CCC	10–13%	530–1,039

Source: BoA Merrill Lynch High Yield Bond Indices. Used by permission.

You should buy or own Strong-Horse companies when spreads are at the widest level (lowest prices), and you should not own the bonds when the spreads are tight, that is, when the yields are low and the prices high. For example, in February 2011, expected default rates were low, the spreads were too tight, and the yields were too low. Tight spreads, good earnings, and a low default environment is not the time to buy. Most likely, a problem will emerge causing spreads to widen, and you will lose money. This is what happened in 2011, when the European debt crisis caused concern in the capital markets and spreads widened. As of February 2012, because the Federal Reserve has pushed Treasury rates down, spreads are at the wide end of the range, but yields are at the low end of the range, making the market acceptable, but only average. You can see this range in Figure 8.1. Buy Strong-Horse companies at wide spreads, not at the tightest spreads.

Figure 8.1 Yield to Maturity Benchmarks*

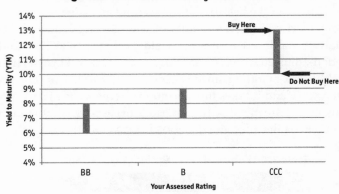

*The yield range, by rating, of the Merrill Lynch Index since December 31, 2003, excluding 2008.
Source: BoA Merrill Lynch High Yield Bond Indices. Used by permission.

Strong-Horse Investing works because you invest in good companies, with solid businesses, manageable debt levels, and a management that honors its bond contracts. Buy the bonds cheaply and earn a good return. You can do this by investing in speculative grade, low rated bonds. You can earn an attractive return buying junk bonds even when you buy bonds at the middle of the range. It is not always possible to buy at the bottom of the market. The middle of the range is adequate. The goal is to pick Strong-Horse companies that will not go bankrupt. For example, with a 3.5% ten-year Treasury, it is quite reasonable to buy an 11.5% CCC bond or an 8% B bond or even a 7% BB bond.

Obviously, buying when the market is down in the face of a credit storm is difficult and requires fortitude. But, if you stick to investing in companies you do think will repay their loans, it is a good strategy. Similarly, it is difficult to not invest when things are rosy. But if spreads are the tightest they have been in eight years, you should think twice.

· WHAT WE KNOW ·

1. To determine if an investment is sound, first perform a Strong-Horse credit analysis to calibrate the rating you think the investment should have.

2. Look at the yield or spread of the investment.

3. If the yield is attractive relative to the creditworthiness, buy it. If not, do not buy it.

4. Do not invest if junk bond spreads are too tight. For example, 200 basis points is too tight.

CHAPTER 9

AN EXAMPLE OF HOW TO CONDUCT A STRONG-HORSE ANALYSIS

In this chapter I conduct an analysis of the packaging industry as an example of how to perform a credit analysis. I have arbitrarily selected the packaging industry; it could have been an analysis of the oil industry, chemical industry, cable industry, or any other. The idea of this analysis is to look at the business and financial risks of the companies within the industry and then to compare these companies to one another.

THE PACKAGING INDUSTRY

Beer, cereal, soda, or just about any other product has to be packaged and shipped before being sold. Packaging mediums include glass, plastic, metal, or paper. While many of the companies have been in the business for years, they have undergone substantial change. Also, competition from product substitution often plays an important role in growth. Over time, for example, beer and soda glass bottles lost ground to aluminum cans. Each material has a specific cost structure that sometimes impacts the volume of its sales. The beer, soda, and other customers are extremely cost conscious, so if one company can charge less than another, it often gets the business.

CONDUCTING A CREDIT ANALYSIS

The following procedure is a step-by-step approach for conducting a detailed credit analysis.

Step 1. Financial Data

Let's look at Owens-Illinois (O-I) as an example:

1. Go to the Securities and Exchange (SEC) website: www.sec.gov.

2. Select "Search for Company Filings" under the Filings and Forms section header.

3. Select "Company or fund name . . ." for search method.

4. Enter the company name (for example, "Owens-Illinois").

5. From the search results, select your desired company.

6. See the list of filings. We often use the 10-Ks (annual reports), 10-Qs (quarterly reports), and some 8-Ks (special filings such as company presentations).

Follow these steps for all the companies you are interested in. Price information also comes from the SEC Financial Industry Regulatory Authority (FINRA, www.finra.org) database. I have created a comparative table of credit and price information (see Table 9.4) for nine packaging companies:

- Berry Plastics

- Graham Packaging

- Solo Cup

- Ball Corporation

- Crown Holdings

- Owens-Illinois (O-I)

- Graphic Packaging

- Rock-Tenn

- Silgan

I have graphed representative bond yields of each packaging company against its S&P bond rating in Figure 9.1.

Figure 9.1 Packaging Yield to Worst Versus S&P Credit Rating, as of September 2010

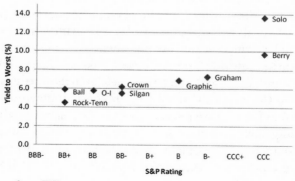

Source: FINRA.

Figure 9.1 is a picture of the yield to worst versus the S&P rating. Notice how the yields trend higher as the quality of the bonds decreases. As explained in this chapter, Solo's yield is much greater than a CCC+-rated bond should be. All information is as of September 2010.

At 14%, Solo Cup is yielding far more than the bonds of the other packaging companies. (Its dollar price is $87.) It also has a lower credit rating than all the others except Berry Plastics. Notice that Solo Cup yields nearly 14% while Owens-Illinois (O-I) yields only 6%. Is Solo Cup a good bond to own because it yields substantially more than O-I?

Step 2. Business Model and Business Risk

Let's take a look at the Owens-Illinois *business model* and *business risk*.

Business Model

Owens-Illinois (O-I) is a BB-rated public company with $7 billion in revenue. It is an international manufacturer of glass packaging primarily for food and beverage products. Its products include glass containers for beer, soft drinks, wine, juice, food, and pharmaceuticals, among others. With manufacturing plants in 21 countries, O-I is the largest glass container producer in the world. It is also the technology leader in its processes.

Solo Cup is a CCC-rated $1.5 billion manufacturer and marketer of single-use products for the food service industry and individual consumers. It produces items such as cups, lids, food containers, bowls, plates, and cutlery in a variety of materials—plastic, paper, foam, and others. Founded in 1936, Solo's product innovation has earned Solo its legacy in the packaging industry. In 2009, 81% of Solo's revenue came from food service customers, while the remaining 19% came from individual "consumer" customers. Solo is a private company owned by the Hulseman family, the founders, and 30+% by the private equity company Vestar Capital Partners.

Business Risk

The size, growth, and trend of the companies are shown in Tables 9.1 and 9.2. All things being equal, I believe bigger credits are better bond investments than smaller credits; they have greater resources and flexibility to weather a downturn. That is one of the reasons I like O-I with sales at $7 billion. Tables 9.1 through 9.3 are a snapshot of O-I's and Solo Cup's 2009 revenue and EBITDA and financial ratios. Notice that both companies had declining margins during this time period.

O-I's sales declined in 2009 and in the first nine months of 2010. The 2010 decline was primarily due to the loss of revenue from the expropriation of its Venezuelan operations. Also, in 2009 the strength of the dollar caused foreign currency loss adjustments. I am impressed with O-I's long history and

Table 9.1 Owens-Illinois Financial Trends (in Millions of Dollars)

	2007	2008	2009	FIRST 9 MONTHS 2009	FIRST 9 MONTHS 2010
Revenue	$7,567	$7,885	$7,067	$5,201	$5,035
EBITDA	$2,298	$1,216	$917	$959	$1,026
Margin	30.4%	15.4%	13.0%	18.0%	20.0%
Adjusted EBITDA	$1,410	$1,496	$1,290	$1,073	$955
Margin	18.6%	19.0%	18.2%	20.6%	19.8%
Leverage*	1.3x	2.4x	3.6x	3.7x	4.1x
Coverage	6.6x	4.8x	4.1x	5.3x	6.0x

*The first 9 months' leverage is instead calculated using last 12 months' (LTM) data.
Source: Company disclosures.

Table 9.2 Solo Cup Financial Trends (in Millions of Dollars)

	2007	2008	2009	FIRST 9 MONTHS 2009	2010
Revenue	$2,110	$1,847	$1,503	$1,116	$1,174
EBITDA	$227	$129	$91	$61	$50
Margin	10.8%	7.0%	6.1%	5.5%	4.3%
Adjusted EBITDA	$146	$152	$129	$97	$68
Margin	6.9%	8.2%	8.6%	8.7%	5.8%
Leverage*	3.3X	5.6x	7.0x	5.7x	9. 0x
Coverage	2.8X	2.1x	1.4X	1.3x	0.9X

*The first 9 months' leverage is instead calculated using last 12 months' (LTM) data.
Source: Company disclosures.

Table 9.3: LTM 9/30/10 Financial Ratios

	LEVEARGE	COVERAGE
Owens-Illinois	4.1x	4.2x
Solo Cup	9.0x	1.1x

its large size. I am not impressed, however, with the negative trend, despite the good reasons for it. O-I's 2007 margins were excellent for the packaging industry. While 2009 saw a dip to its lowest point, 2010 margins look to be regaining some traction and are still very good compared to competitors.

Solo Cup has experienced declining revenue and profitability over the past three years, and for the first nine months in 2010, it had a net loss of $87 million, along with a decline in its EBITDA. In its presentation materials to investors, Solo indicated its turnaround plans included consolidating manufacturing costs and increasing operational efficiency. Between 2007 and 2009, revenues declined nearly 30%, but they have stabilized in the first nine months of 2010. The company's EBITDA, however, fell 36% in 2009 and again during the first nine months of 2010. The trend is terrible. Business risk is high. The company must stabilize its earnings. (I hope it works.) Unlike O-I, Solo's margins have remained in steady decline over the past few years. While Solo's margins were never too impressive, they reached a point of concern during the past year.

Step 3. Financial Risk

O-I's balance sheet is closer to a BB credit than a single B credit. While its leverage is a little high (see Table 9.1), its coverage is good. Both ratios are healthy for the industry: not too much debt while easily able to cover its interest expense. Also, O-I's coverage improved while its leverage increased. The increase in leverage, while not good, was at a conservative level. Solo's ratios are troublesome. Solo had 1.1 times coverage over the last 12 months ending September 30, 2010, meaning it barely generated enough cash flow to pay its interest obligations. Its leverage was 8.9 times, meaning that its debt was about 9 times its cash flow—far too high.

Solo Cup statistics are so bad that if management cannot turn the company around, the price could fall precipitously from the current levels. In my opinion, it is too risky an investment at this time. Many hedge funds may already be short the bond, anticipating future problems.

Solo Cup is cheap, but it could get cheaper (its price could drop further). While it is a substantial company, business and financial risks are high and worsening. If the company cannot regroup and improve, it could go bankrupt. I would not buy the bonds. As I was writing this book, Standard & Poor's lowered its rating from CCC+ to CCC. Its price dropped three points.

O-I is a much bigger, stronger, and better capitalized company. Its interest is well covered at 4.2 times, and its leverage is acceptable. While we would like to see improving financials, the bonds are safe. From a credit perspective, it is a Strong-Horse company. Its chances of defaulting are low. For investment grade investors willing to take a little credit risk or for pension funds needing to match a liability with higher yielding assets, this company is a legitimate alternative.

The junk bond market has risen nearly 80% since the beginning of 2009 to December 2010. I would be surprised if there were any bargains at this late stage of the recovery. Our goal is to avoid potential problem credits such as Solo Cup and to avoid credits where there is limited upside potential and some downside risk in the event that the bond market rises in yield and declines in price. Unfortunately, this risk is reflected in O-I's very low yield to worst call of 6%. I do not think the company can get upgraded by the rating agencies until it starts showing revenue and profit growth. As such, its bond yield and price will be more subject to "bond math" than to credit arbitrage.

Rising interest rates and Treasury rates, often associated with an improving economy, are bad for all bonds, especially the lower yielding, higher quality bonds. For instance, in 1994, the Federal Reserve increased the fed funds rate 250 bp and caused bond prices to fall. All bond prices, including junk bond prices, fell. However, the higher yielding, higher coupon bonds fell the least because more of the return came from the higher coupon and the improved economy increased the chances of a debt ratings upgrade. O-I is neither high yielding nor (in my opinion) an upgrade candidate. Given that at the time of this writing the economy is starting to grow and the expectation is for increased Federal Reserve activity, I can recommend the purchase of this high quality company only as an alternative to investment grade possibilities.

A financial comparison of the nine different companies in the packaging industry is seen in Table 9.4. The table is called a *comp sheet*. It is easier to compare the financial data and the ratios of companies when they are looked at side-by-side in a single table. This comparison can simplify a sea of numbers and help investors make informed decisions. The comp sheet contains representative bond information (rating, price, yield, and maturity) and credit statistics (leverage, coverage, size, and trend).

· WHAT WE KNOW ·

1. The analysis of the packaging industry is an example of how to conduct a detailed credit analysis.

2. The SEC databases can provide both the credit and price information you need to perform a credit analysis and an investment analysis.

3. Make this comparison for all the companies you are interested in comparing. I have presented this comparison in the form of a comp sheet in Table 9.4 and a graph in Figure 9.1.

4. The highest yielding investment is often too risky. The yield can rise further, that is, the price can fall further. The lowest yielding investment may also be too rich and not a good investment.

Table 9.4 Comp Sheet

ISSUER NAME	BERRY PLASTICS	GRAHAM PACKAGING	SOLO CUP	BALL CORP
DEBT AND PRICING STATISTICS				
Coupon	9.75	8.25	8.50	7.38
Maturity	1/15/21	10/1/18	2/15/14	9/1/19
Callable	Yes	Yes	Yes	Yes
Moody's	Caa1	Caa1	Caa2	Ba1
S&P	CCC	B-	CCC	BB+
Fitch	—	CCC	CCC	BB
Price	$100.00	$104.30	$87.38	$107.75
Yield to Worst (%)	9.7	7.3	13.6	5.9
Spread (bp)	609	420	1201	259
OPERATING STATISTICS				
9 Months 10 Rev	$3,103	$1,869	$1,174	$5,635
9 Months 09 Rev	$2,393	$1,736	$1,116	$4,983
09 Rev	$3,187	$2,271	$1,503	$7,345
08 Rev	$3,513	$2,559	$1,847	$7,562
07 Rev	$3,055	$2,471	$2,110	$7,390
9 Months 10 EBITDA	$383	$267	$50	$825
9 Months 09 EBITDA	$344	$329	$61	$692
9 Months 10 Adj EBITDA	$436	$314	$68	$770
9 Months 09 Adj EBITDA	$350	$348	$97	$676
09 EBITDA	$466	$378	$91	$953
08 EBITDA	$369	$313	$129	$902
07 EBITDA	$255	$223	$227	$807
09 Adj EBITDA	$474	$443	$129	$945
08 Adj EBITDA	$411	$427	$152	$933
07 Adj EBITDA	$375	$410	$146	$840
EBITDA MARGIN				
EBITDA Margin	12.3%	14.3%	4.3%	14.6%
Adj EBITDA Margin	14.0%	16.8%	5.8%	13.7%
LEVERAGE				
Long-Term Debt	$4,404	$2,814	$718	$2,055
Debt/LTM EBITDA	8.7x	8.9x	8.9x	1.9x
Debt/LTM Adj EBITDA	7.9x	6.9x	7.2x	2.0x
COVERAGE				
LTM Interest Exp	$284	$181	$70	$145
LTM EBITDA/Int Exp	1.8x	1.8x	1.1x	7.5x
LTM Adj EBITDA/Int Exp	2.0x	2.3x	1.4x	7.2x
CAPITAL EXPENDITURE				
9 Months 10 CapEx	$171.4	$111.2	$37.7	$131.1
9 Months 09 CapEx	$144.2	$104.5	$52.7	$117.0
9 Months 10 EBITDA-CapEx	$211.6	$155.8	$12.3	$693.9
9 Months 09 EBITDA-CapEx	$199.8	$224.5	$8.3	$575.0

Source: Company disclosures.

CROWN HOLDINGS	OWENS-ILLINOIS	GRAPHIC PACKAGING	ROCK-TENN	SILGAN
7.75	7.38	7.88	9.25	7.25
11/15/15	5/15/16	10/1/28	3/15/16	8/15/16
Yes	No	Yes	Yes	Yes
—	Ba3	B3	Ba2	Ba3
BB-	BB	B	BB+	BB-
—	BB+	B	—	—
$103.78	$107.36	$104.50	$109.97	$107.00
6.2	5.8	6.9	4.5	5.5
409	331	380	201	301
5,992	$5,035	$3,083	$2,195	$2,360
$6,021	$5,201	$3,117	$2,083	$2,361
$7,938	$7,067	$4,096	$2,812	$3,067
$8,305	$7,885	$4,079	$2,839	$3,121
$7,727	$7,567	$2,421	$2,316	$2,923
$697	$992	$373	$364	$349
$655	$930	$440	$408	$357
$710	$995	$432	$371	$357
$684	$1,073	$404	$423	$359
$782	$917	$583	$513	$443
$856	$1,216	$416	$561	$398
$675	$2,298	$312	$346	$404
$853	$1,290	$523	$523	$445
$910	$1,496	$451	$565	$410
$795	$1,410	$314	$346	$410
11.6%	19.7%	12.1%	16.6%	14.8%
11.8%	19.8%	14.0%	16.9%	15.1%
$2,774	$4,006	$2,697	$897	$892
3.4x	4.1x	5.2x	1.9x	2.1x
3.2x	3.3x	4.9x	1.9x	2.0x
$205	$234	$172	$81	$59
4.0x	4.2x	3.0x	5.8x	7.4x
4.3x	5.2x	3.2x	5.8x	7.5x
$187.0	$391.6	$73.9	$60.9	$76.0
$108.0	$193.7	$96.3	$49.3	$72.1
$510.0	$600.4	$299.1	$303.1	$273.0
$547.0	$736.3	$343.7	$358.7	$284.9

CHAPTER 10

BONDHOLDERS VERSUS STOCKHOLDERS AND THE JUNK BOND ADVANTAGE

Understanding the difference between the risks and rewards that accrue to bond and stock investors is fundamental to success in bond investing. When you buy a bond of a company, you are lending that company money. You expect to receive semi-annual interest and your principal back at the maturity of the bond. If a company performs better than expected, often the bond price will rise because the probability that you will receive your money back has improved. Conversely, if a company performs worse than expected, the bond price will drop because the probability that you will receive your money back has declined. It is important to realize that you will not get anything more than par ($1,000) in most cases at maturity.

When you own a share of stock, you are an owner of that company. If the company performs poorly, the value of your shares should fall, and if the company performs well, the share price should reflect that and rise.

Owning stocks is risky, and junk bonds compare favorably. For example, returning to my son's $1,000, if he buys four shares of Apple, Inc. ($250 each at the time of this writing), he is an owner of the company. The head of the company and his management team are working for my son. They *must* do everything in their power to protect and hopefully grow the company so that the stock price can rise. The previous CEO, Steve Jobs, did a great job at Apple before passing away in October 2011. With Jobs at the helm, the value of Apple stock rose substantially between 2000 and 2010 (Figure 10.1).

Had my son bought shares in a different company, say, General Motors, three years ago, he would have lost most, or all, of his money, and a Florida vacation would have been a better option (Figure 10.2).

There are many strategies for picking stocks. I subscribe to the theory of investing in good companies at a cheap price. (I strongly recommend Joel Greenblatt's book *The Little Book*

Figure 10.1 Apple Equity Price January 3, 2000, to July 19, 2010

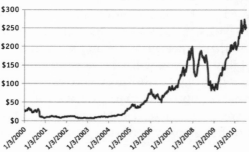

Figure 10.2 General Motors Equity Price
January 3, 2000, to July 19, 2010

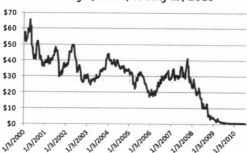

That Still Beats the Markets on this topic [Wiley, New York, 2010].) This approach has been written about by Benjamin Graham and David Dodd in *Security Analysis* (McGraw-Hill, New York, 1934). And it has been successfully executed by Warren Buffett, the driving force behind the phenomenal success at Berkshire Hathaway.

The analysis of a company's performance for both a stock and bond is virtually the same, but the emphasis is different. For example, a company has a new product that can generate huge profits if successful but the probability of success is low. That might make a good stock investment, but it would not be a sound bond investment. Remember, as a shareholder, you share in the value of the growth in the company; as a bondholder, you just want your money back.

Management teams cannot be fiduciaries to both shareholders and bondholders. They can be a fiduciary to only one party, the shareholder. Bondholders have to protect themselves, and we do so by insisting on a strong contract. The terms of that contract are called *covenants*, and they are contained in an *indenture*.

Bondholders need the strongest possible covenants to protect themselves (and I devote all of Chapter 17 to covenants). One way of succeeding in high yield investing is by not taking large risks. Just say no! (You'll notice I repeat that mantra as we go along.)

Oftentimes a company's management will transfer wealth from bondholders to shareholders. They can do it legally by staying within the scope of the narrowly defined covenants. Here are some examples:

1. Paying a large dividend to shareholders, not from earnings but from cash on hand

2. Borrowing money to pay a large dividend

3. Spinning out subsidiaries to shareholders and keeping all the debt in the company to which you lent money

4. Buying back stock in a significant way

Let's return to the yellow pages directory business to show an example of this transfer of wealth. As discussed, at one time, yellow pages were profitable with sales and earnings growing consistently. Customers' usage declined, however, as Internet directories for phone numbers became more popular. Verizon anticipated this declining trend and spun off its yellow pages business to shareholders (the company is called Idearc). Qwest Communications sold its yellow pages business to private equity buyers. Those private equity firms raised debt levels to first buy the company and then again to pay themselves a dividend. Subsequently, sales and earnings fell, and the high debt load became too much. The company filed for Chapter 11 bankruptcy. Bondholders suffered huge losses, but the new shareholders had the huge dividend to protect themselves.

Since there is a risk of a company not being able to pay back its debt (also called *defaulting*), the company pays investors interest on the borrowed money. Naturally, the riskier the investment, the higher the interest rate of the bond. For example, take a company such as Exxon Mobil, the oil and gas giant. Chances are that Exxon Mobil will continue to operate and be profitable for years to come. Therefore, the company's bonds will pay a lower interest rate compared to a riskier company such as the Neiman Marcus Group, the upscale retail company. Exxon Mobil is rated AAA, and Neiman Marcus is rated CCC+. After a tough year of sales and a tremendous operating loss, Neiman Marcus's bonds are considered relatively risky investments. After another year of lackluster sales, the company may not have the cash to pay back its bondholders, justifying a higher interest rate. Thus, $1,000 of Exxon Mobil bonds yields only 4½% and has less risk than Neiman Marcus bonds, which yield roughly 9% and have a greater risk of default.

Stock investors look for capital gains and dividends. Certainly dividends are important, particularly when Treasury rates are less than dividend rates, but capital gains are a substantial portion of the return. Bond investors, on the other hand, rely on the semiannual coupon to provide the bulk of returns.

THE ANATOMY OF A BOND

When a company issues a bond, it pays a coupon (interest payment) twice a year, and the bond matures after a certain time. For example, if you have an 8% coupon on a five-year bond, you would receive 10 semiannual coupons at 4% each. A new issue bond *yield* is the coupon when the bond is issued at $1,000 per bond (called "100" for 100 cents on the dollar).

The convention is to describe the bond with the company's ticker symbol. For example, if Millie's company (ticker: MIL) issued bonds with an annual coupon of 8% that mature December 10, 2017, in the bond world, this is how that would be written:

MIL 8   12/10/2017

If the bond price falls to 80 ($800 per bond) and you buy it five years before maturity, your yield grows to 13.7%. You would receive two coupons every year (semiannually) and a $200 capital gain at maturity, that is, $1,000 at maturity, which is $200 more than you paid for it. Your return is the present value of your receipts divided by your cost. Therefore, your bond's yield to maturity is 13.7%. (*Note:* Assume that the Treasury debt security with the same maturity yields 3%.) Thus your spread is 1,370 − 300 = 1,070 bp.

As the price declined from 100 to 80, the yield increased from 8% to 13.7%. When prices drop, yields rise and vice versa. The relationship is calculated as a *yield to maturity* (YTM) *calculation*. You can calculate the YTM on most financial calculators or with Excel:

You pay at initiation	$800
Annual coupon rate	8%
Frequency of payments	Semiannually
Length until maturity	5 years
You will receive	$1,000
Yield to maturity	13.65%
Spread maturity	1,070 bp

Figure 10.3 Yield to Maturity (YTM) of the MIL Bond

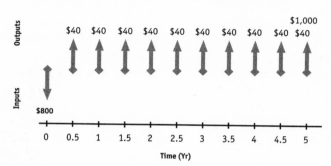

In Figure 10.3, you pay $800 today and receive $1,000 five years from now. You also receive 10 payments of $40 each. The present value of the $40 coupons is about $283, and the present value of the $1,000 payment in five years is worth about $517.

THE JUNK BOND ADVANTAGE

The coupon stream becomes more valuable as the interest rate or the number of payments increases. This is the junk bond advantage. You can mathematically get 10%, 30%, or even upward of 50% more on your investment in certain circumstances with junk bonds over what you would get from investment grade bonds. Let me illustrate.

According to Table 5.1 (in Chapter 5), 10-year, AA-rated bonds were yielding 3.4% while B-rated bonds were yielding 8.8%—a 5.4% difference. Suppose we bought 10-year AA- and B-rated bonds at par. The yield equals the coupon rate, as we bought the bonds at par. The AA-rated bond's coupon payments are $34 per year while the B-rated bond's coupon payments are $88 per year. The difference is $54 per year, a 158% advantage in current yield for the B-rated bond. That difference is the junk bond advantage. Compounding that advantage over the life of the bonds can result in an enormous extra return to junk bond investors. For example, assuming that you can reinvest at the same rates, the AA-rated bond's future value in 10 years will be $1,401, while the B-rated bond's future value will be $2,366.

This example assumes that neither of the bonds defaults. While we know that junk bonds are at greater risk of default than investment grade bonds, properly selecting a high yield bond can use the junk bond advantage to its full potential. In today's market, coupon advantage is the reason why junk bonds are so popular in low interest rate countries such as the United States and Japan.

The junk bond market can often lead the stock market down. During recessionary times, corporate earnings and cash flows decline, which scares bond investors. They run for the exits, trying to sell their bonds quickly, causing bond prices to drop and bond spreads to widen. Companies need to access the debt markets and conduct business. When liquidity dries up in both the bond and bank markets, companies can fail. When a company does not pay full interest and principal, stock investors get wiped out. Understanding what's happening in the junk bond market can give equity investors insight into when to exit their stock holdings.

· WHAT WE KNOW ·

1. Bond and stock investors who invest in the same company can be at odds with one another.

2. Business risk analysis is the same for both stock and bond investors. Look for large growing companies that are not highly leveraged.

3. A management team can be a fiduciary only to shareholders. Bondholders have to look out for themselves.

4. The only protection bondholders have is a contract known as an *indenture*. Understanding that contract is important.

5. The junk bond advantage is a high coupon paid over several years.

CHAPTER 11

MANAGEMENT AND OWNERSHIP

One of the first lessons I learned about investing was that management counts. The right management team can enhance shareholder value and protect bondholder loans. Owning a company, however, is like sleeping with management. There is a saying on Wall Street: "If you sleep with dogs, then you are bound to get fleas."

Do not sleep with, or invest in, companies whose managers you are not 100% sure will be honorable and knowledgeable. Part of Strong-Horse Investing is picking the right team. If you invest in a company and it defaults, shame on that company. If you invest in that company, with the same management, a second time and it defaults again, shame on you. The junk bond industry is rife with managers who constantly default and industries that are serial defaulters. Here are two examples of new issue bond deals that I believe you should *not* invest in.

The owner of several casinos on the East Coast has defaulted more than once. He has overleveraged his casinos, underspent on maintaining them, and is constantly in litigation with coinvestors and lenders (or at least threatening them with litigation). In the past he has tried to avoid making interest payments while requesting that lenders not declare it an event of default.

Another example of an issue bond deal to avoid can be found in my personal experience. Representatives of a Native American–run casino once came to me for a loan while I was working at Nomura. The chief of the tribe was $1/32$ Native American, and he was pumping gas prior to being approached by developers to build an "Indian casino" in a prosperous location. While the tribe retained an experienced management team, the owners were inexperienced. They came to my office, and the chief said that even though there was no tangible property, no revenue yet, and the deal had poor covenants, we had his word that he would repay the loan. The bonds are currently trading at distressed levels. Furthermore, the details on how a Native American business bankruptcy on tribal land will be handled in bankruptcy court are murky.

Between defaults and overleveraged operations with the East Coast casinos and lack of experience, revenue, and tangible property with the Native American venture, it would have been a poor decision to invest in either of these operations. Both were obviously facing major management issues. The business owner and management team are vital to the success of your bond investment. Analysts often debate the importance of actually meeting management before making an investment (stock or bond). Some analysts declare they won't make an investment unless they have met management and have been able to ask questions about business strategies and the competitive landscape. Other analysts say meeting management is unnecessary, pointing out that when management responds with important information, they more often than not tilt their response to meet their objectives anyhow. This second group would rather analyze the financial statements and deduce a conclusion. Surprisingly, both positions are right but not for obvious reasons.

It is now possible to research the Internet for information on management or buyout groups. At a minimum, you should understand management's philosophy relating to corporate strategy. If you have the opportunity to meet management, do not be deceived by appearances. How someone looks or acts often influences our perceptions, especially in the arts or politics, but you should not let it influence your investments. Should you avoid investing in a company because the CEO is bald? How about if she has a full head of hair? In my view, a CEO's looks are unimportant—an analyst has to get below surface appearances.

The *only* reason to meet management is to decide if the issuer is a company you should *not invest in*. Do not invest in any company because you met the management and were suitably impressed. Look for reasons not to invest. If management has done things that leave you unsure, *do not* invest. If management does not know the business, *do not* invest.

For example, I met with the management of a private equity company that was acquiring a drug distribution company. This company's largest numbers of employees were in the sales department, and their biggest expenses were being spent on the sales force. They essentially were taking a large number of drugs and distributing them in different market channels (for example, TV, doctor direct sales, and publications). I asked the new CEO how his sales force was organized, and he did not know. His response was a warning signal that the company was not ready for investment.

Another time, I met with the new CEO of a successful chemical company. He was a relative of the founder, had recently been given the job, and was in my office raising money for that business. Our chemical analyst asked the question, "How much of your revenue increase was price appreciation, and how much was volume increase?" This information is a basic bit of knowledge any CEO should know, but he did not.

Remember, management of a solvent company has no fiduciary duty to lenders, only to shareholders. Oftentimes we want the managers, or owners, to have an investment in the company so that they have an incentive to succeed. However, this situation also could be a problem if they take nefarious actions to pump up the value of their stock at the expense of their debt. The managers could backdate stock options, taking money from the corporation and giving it to themselves. The management also could add debt to buy up stock, reducing the creditworthiness of the company. This move is often done and can be stopped only with good covenants.

It is amazing to me how the same players continuously show up in this market time and time again. Private equity issuers such as Apollo, Blackstone, and Kohlberg Kravis Roberts (KKR) continuously issue debt. These entities have been doing this since the 1970s, and maybe before. Some of their deals have worked out, and others have not. A student of this market gets to understand the financing philosophies of each of these parties. It scares me when I see some of the newer fund managers in their twenties negotiating with these masters. It is like a high school wrestler competing against an Olympic champion, using the Olympian's wrestling rules.

· WHAT WE KNOW ·

1. Management and ownership are important; they could make the difference between a successful and an unsuccessful investment.

2. Be warned. If the owners or managers did something once to extract additional value for themselves at bondholder expense, they could do it again.

3. Private equity deals reduce the creditworthiness of existing companies. They often put too much debt on a company and the company could default.

4. The only reason to meet management is to look for reasons not to invest.

5. Bald-headed managers can be quite good.

CHAPTER 12

BOND PRICE VOLATILITY

Which of the following statements is false?

A. Owning a junk bond is safe.

B. Bond prices never change much.

C. Bond volatility is greater than stock volatility.

D. The Brooklyn Bridge is for sale.

The answer: all of the above.

Junk bond prices fluctuate a lot. Sometimes they rise and fall for fundamental credit reasons, and other times they rise and fall for technical reasons. Some technical reasons include supply and demand or a large market selloff. Bond prices change for liquidity reasons as well. Sometimes bonds fall for a combination of all three: credit, technicals, and liquidity. Investment grade bond volatility is less than junk bond volatility, which is less than stock volatility. For those people conversant with bond fundamentals and technical considerations, volatility can be your friend. And, despite many jokes to the contrary, the Brooklyn Bridge is not for sale.

VALUING A BOND

What is the difference between a bond and a teenage boy? Bonds mature. (That was to get your attention; the next sentence is actually important.) Bonds mature and stocks do not, so *it is easier to value a bond than a stock.*

Here is a tough question. I am going to offer you two choices, and you must select the better investment:

1. $1,000 in cash 10 years from now

2. A $1,000 corporate bond today, 0% coupon, that matures 10 years from now, and you know nothing about the creditworthiness of the company

Which would you choose? The correct answer: *take the cash.* We do not know anything about the company, and the price of the bond in the future could be less than it is today, but it cannot be more. This choice displays the risk inherent in bond price volatility.

The price of a bond at maturity is $1,000 per bond. If the bond matures, you will be repaid $1,000. The only way to get less than $1,000 at that time is if it defaults—in which case you get paper of a defaulted company that typically is worth far less than par. The value of a stock at any time is based on assumption, analysis, and current events—it does not mature. For that reason, it is easier to value a bond than a stock. For junk bonds the main determinant of value is based on creditworthiness.

You have to conduct a credit analysis to determine the probability of default. If the default probability of a company

Figure 12.1 General Motors Stock Versus Bond Prices

increases, the yield of that company's bonds should increase and the price of the bonds should decrease, and vice versa. Each quarter, a company reports its performance. If the performance is so good that the probability of default is lower than before, the bond price should rise. If a company takes on substantial debt that reduces the creditworthiness of the company, the bond price should fall. Both stocks and bonds move up and down. Especially when the creditworthiness is declining, price declines of both the bonds and stocks move in tandem. An example is General Motors' declining creditworthiness (due to declining market share and lost sales), which harmed both the bond and stock prices, illustrated in Figure 12.1.

WHY VOLATILITY IS A WIDELY USED MEASURE OF RISK

Changes in credit quality determine bond price movement, and changes in the economic environment determine the volatility of the asset class. *But what is volatility?* An easy way to understand volatility is to look at the recent weather, which in any February can vary from 28°F above average to 15°F below average. Just as the volatility in prevailing weather patterns sometimes results in death and destruction in the affected communities, so too does volatility of securities prices pose a risk to investment performance. The more volatile investment returns are, the more difficult it is to determine what your returns will be.

This is a test question: Would you prefer to always have a 12% return each year (Strategy 1), or would you prefer to have a return of 12% on average (Strategy 2)? Sometimes it is zero, or negative, and sometimes it is more than 12%. I would prefer the constant 12% return. You can see that graphically in Figure 12.2.

Figure 12.2 shows the end-of-month cumulative returns for our two investment strategies. Strategy 1 yielded a consistent 1% return each month, accumulating a 12% return by the end of the year. Strategy 2 was much less predictable and much more volatile than Strategy 1: it returned 0% in January and 4% in February, and then it lost 3% in March, leaving a 1% return after the first three months of the year—compared to a 3% return with Strategy 1. By the end of April, however, Strat-

Figure 12.2 End-of-Month Cumulative Returns*

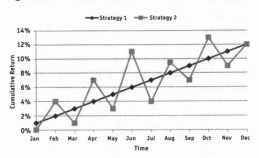

*For illustrative purposes. Assume rounding at all times.

egy 1 had returned 4%—compared to 7% by Strategy 2—after a strong 6% return in April. As you can see, this pattern continues for the rest of the year until they both finish with a 12% return. While the end result is the same (12%), Strategy 1's consistent, reliable returns show that it is less volatile and therefore a less risky invesment than Strategy 2.

In July Strategy 2 lost nearly 7%, and had we sold our investment, we would not have achieved the same results as the constant return. However, if we decided to sell in August, we would have outperformed the constant return. Thus, investment Strategy 2 has the same returns as Strategy 1, but it is undoubtedly more risky.

Note that Strategy 1 has zero volatility. It has a 1% return each period. Strategy 2 has a calculated volatility measure of 5%. It is calculated as the standard deviation of returns. A larger number means greater variation in returns.The volatile strategy is riskier because you are not certain of what your return will be. The bond return range goes up and down a greater amount. It is far more volatile than Strategy 1. (See the Appendix for the calculation of volatility.)

Figure 12.3 plots the returns of the S&P 500 Index, the BoA Merrill Lynch High Yield Index (HUC0),[1] and the Strong-Horse Method for the years 1992 through 2009. It is interesting to note that the stock market, as measured by the S&P 500 Index, had a lower return and greater volatility than both the high yield index and the Strong-Horse measures. The calculated volatility of the annual returns of each is shown below:

S&P 500 Index	20.0%
BoA Merrill Lynch HY Index	16.8%
Strong-Horse Method	18.6%

Figure 12.3 Comparable Annual Returns for 1992 through 2009

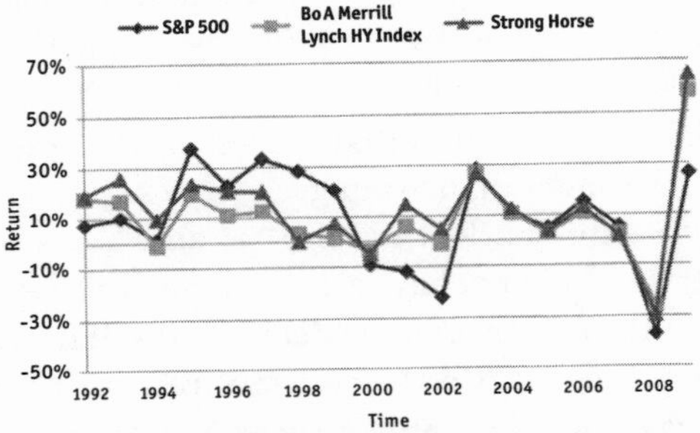

Source: BoA Merrill Lynch High Yield Bond Indices and Nomura Corporate Research and Asset Management, High Yield Total Return Institutional Composite (HYTRIC). Used by permission.

Spread Volatility

We saw in Chapter 6 that bond prices and yields are mathematically equivalent. But spreads, calculated by subtracting the appropriate maturity Treasury from yield, are used more frequently to reflect changes in credit quality. When credit or other problems occur, spreads widen (prices fall), and when there is a perceived improvement in the investment climate, spreads tighten (prices rise). Spreads widen and tighten; cycles of widening and tightening have occurred often, and these cycles seem to be repeating with greater frequency over the past 35 years. Recessions tend to result in high levels of credit problems and defaults, which widen spreads. What happens during a recession is that sales, margins, earnings, cash flow, and financial ratios all decline. As a result credit ratings fall, spreads widen, and bond prices decline.

The Strong-Horse Method will help you take advantage of spread and price volatility.

Figure 12.4 is a plot of the BoA Merrill Lynch High Yield Bond Index spreads since the end of 1996. Spreads peaked at more than 2,000 bp (20%) in 2008, and they were as narrow as mid-300 bp (3%) one year earlier. Excluding the market collapse in 2008, the range was between 300 and 1,000 bp. Recessionary periods are highlighted in the figure. The lighter shade illustrates the selloff, and the darker shade is the recovery. Market dynamics such as supply and demand, the economy, and default rates increase market volatility. The market has always come back, and not all companies default. During a market selloff, the strong credits decline in price in line with those that will default. The Strong-Horse Method helps you find the good companies, those that can withstand a downturn—if you buy them at low prices, they generate a high return.

Figure 12.4 BoA Merrill Lynch High Yield Bond Index Spreads Since the End of 1996

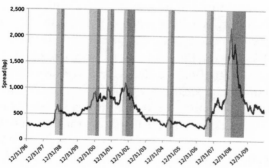

Spreads, in this context, refer to *option-adjusted spreads* (OASs). The OAS is the spread between the relevant bond and its equivalent maturity treasury.

Recessionary periods are highlighted. The lighter shade illustrates the selloff, and the darker shade illustrates the recovery.

Source: BoA Merrill Lynch High Yield Bond Indices. Used by permission.

Type I and Type II Errors

In bond analysis, as opposed to equity analysis, the risk/reward dynamics are much different when you miss a good investment from when you make a bad one. I call the errors of making a bad investment Type I, and the errors of missing a good investment Type II. If you own a par bond and it runs into credit problems, the bond price could drop 50 points. If you miss a par investment that does well, you could have missed a 10-point (10%) rise. Thus, one Type I error is equal to five Type II errors. I never bemoan the fact that I missed a good investment. Before buying a junk bond, take the time to perform a good credit analysis. You make money by not making mistakes. In bond investing, defense wins.

Liquidity

Credit is the most important factor in junk bond volatility. But liquidity is a close second. Supply and demand dictate high yield bond transaction prices. If no broker wants to buy my bonds, even though the credit is good, the bond price will fall. This situation is called a *liquidity event*, and it happens often. Paradoxically, for junk bonds, in such instances the best (biggest, most liquid) credits drop the most in price. This drop occurs because the bonds are the only ones brokers are willing to trade in a crisis. The other bonds cannot trade, and thus their reported prices change less. That's what happened in the 2007 to 2008 market meltdown: it overreacted on the downside.

Principal Versus Agency Transactions

Trading a stock is different from trading a bond. A stock is traded on an exchange, and your broker charges a commission. With a bond, on the other hand, your brokerage firm uses its own money to buy the bond from you and then resells that bond, typically at a higher price, giving it a profit. A bond transaction is a *principal transaction*. A stock purchase or sale is an *agency transaction*. Big buyers and sellers of bonds usually get a better price than the little guy because of the huge volume.

Price transparency is greater for stocks because the trades are conducted publicly on the exchanges. Only recently has the Financial Industry Regulatory Authority (FINRA), the government regulator, started reporting bond trades on its website (it is a step in the right direction and should be enhanced). Nevertheless, these reports have greatly improved junk bond price transparency. It is now easy to access bond prices (and other data) through FINRA's Market Data Center website, and anyone can do so for free. Here's how:

1. Google "FINRA bond prices" to find the website.

2. Select bond type: Treasury, corporate, or municipal.

3. Enter a ticker symbol (for example, S for Sprint Nextel Corporation).

4. For corporate bonds it may be necessary to use the advanced bond search function to locate the appropriate bond.

Note: Some corporate bonds are not easy to find. You may need the security's CUSIP (Committee on Uniform Securities Identification Procedures) number. A CUSIP number is an identification number assigned to all stocks and registered bonds.

A CLEAR EXAMPLE OF VOLATILITY

The best way to demonstrate junk bond volatility is by example. We will discuss the bond price volatility of several corporate issuers in some detail. The first example is Clear Channel Communications (CCU), a radio broadcasting and outdoor billboard advertising company. It is an example of a bond whose price dropped 90+ points before recovering somewhat.

Clear Channel is the largest AM, FM pure play station owner and operator in the United States, with 900 stations. It grew both organically and, especially, through acquisitions. It has several businesses including outdoor advertising (billboards) and concert promotion and hosting. Figure 12.5 shows the price movement of one of Clear Channel's bonds: 6⅞ due 2018. Prior to November 2006, the company was an investment grade credit whose bonds traded near par (100% of its principal or $1,000 per bond). Notice how the price hit a low point at 7.5 cents on the dollar at its trough. What happened?

1. November 16, 2006: CCU entered into a buyout agreement with Bain Capital and Thomas H. Lee Partners.

2. July 30, 2008: The leveraged buyout closed, valuing the company at $24 billion and raising the pro forma (PF) leverage[2] to 9 times.

3. September 15, 2008: Lehman Brothers filed for bankruptcy.

4. March 9, 2009: The BoA Merrill Lynch High Yield Index began to rally; it ended in a 58% return in 2009 (measured by HUC0).

5. December 18, 2009: Clear Channel Outdoor priced $2.5 billion of bonds, which boosted its parent liquidity.

6. August 9, 2010: CCU announced in-line second quarter 2010 results, and the net total leverage was 13.1 times.

Three important events occurred that crushed the bond price; they are illustrated in Figure 12.5. First, it was purchased by two private equity companies: Bain Capital and Thomas H. Lee on November 16, 2006 (on the chart, this is indicated by point 1). This type of purchase added substantial debt on Clear Channel's balance sheet when the purchase was consummated in 2008 (point 2). The debt grew from about $6.5 billion in 2007 to $19.5 billion in 2008. Through financial engineering, the added debt was put on CCU's balance sheet. This added

Figure 12.5 Clear Channel Communications 6.875% due 2018 Bond Price (December 31, 2004, through December 31, 2010)

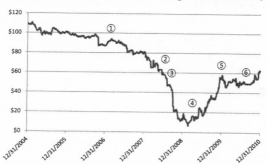

debt requirement in the best of times can be difficult to meet. It was a disastrous time in 2008. The market was experiencing a liquidity event, and capital was scarce. It was more difficult to run the business because the company had to save its cash for interest payments and debt pay-down.

The bond in question (6⅞ due 2018) was typical of investment grade bonds in that it did not have many contractual protections (covenants). Thus, when the private equity buyers (Bain and T.H. Lee) purchased CCU, they ruthlessly "crammed down" the older "legacy" bonds below the billions of dollars of new debt used to buy the company. In the event of a bankruptcy, debt is paid back to bondholders in order of priority based on what type of issue the bond is (senior secured, senior subordinated, and so on). When CCU was bought by Bain and T.H. Lee, the bond issue that was second on the priority list was demoted, or "crammed down," to below the new debt coming into the company. Thus, since that issue now has a lower probability of being paid back, it is a riskier investment: its yield increases while its price decreases. The added debt alone was enough to reduce the creditworthiness and lower the bond price, but the cram-down of the old legacy bonds theoretically lowered the price even more. In the priority of payments, all the buyout debt should get paid before the legacy bonds in the event of default.

It is typical of private equity buyers to pile on debt to the acquired companies to finance the acquisition of these companies. Companies have to save all their nickels and dimes to cover their financial obligations. Often they have to cut back on expansion plans and maintenance. Sometimes they have to fire employees and reduce contributions to pension plans.

The second event that crushed the bond price was the decline of "old technology" such as radio and print advertising.

In the past, companies spent their advertising dollars exclusively on broadcast media and print publications (for example, newspapers and magazines). Now these companies were also spending their advertising dollars for advertising on Internet competitors such as Google, Facebook, and Yahoo!. Many print and broadcast companies consequently suffered substantial revenue and profit declines, and Clear Channel was no exception. In addition to the increased financial risk associated with the huge debt load resulting from the acquisition, the company had substantial business risk arising from the growth of the Internet competitors. Most acquisitions require business growth to pay off the debt. It is a calamity when revenue fundamentally declines due to increased business risk.

Table 12.1 shows the historical revenue, EBITDA (remember this is a profit measure), and total debt for the three years ending 2009. Note that leverage—total debt to EBITDA—grew from 2.5 times, a conservative level (meaning it would take 2.5 years to pay off the debt at current earnings), to 13.5 times. Under most circumstances, this debt level would be too high for the company to survive. If revenues were not declining, it would be problematic; but with revenue declining, it has been a problem for the company. A further review of the 2009 income statements shows that Clear Channel, despite its problems, was able to pay the interest that it owed because of financial engineering and asset sales. However, its debt levels are so high that

Table 12.1 Clear Channel Financials

	2007	2008	2009
Revenue	$6,921.2	$6,688.7	$5,551.9
EBITDA	$2,426.3	$1,955.0	$1,502.1
Total Debt	$6,575.2	$19,503.7	$20,702.0

its business must grow its capital structure to avoid default in the future.

The third negative event (shown in Figure 12.5 at point 3) was the collapse of the capital markets associated with the Lehman Brothers bankruptcy. Companies default for liquidity reasons, not bad performance. Refinancing debt coming due was virtually impossible at that time. A combination of all three events resulted in CCU bonds dropping from 100 to less than 10 cents on the dollar.

As long as the banks will continue to provide liquidity, the company will not default. The collapse of the capital market shut down liquidity, and thus the CCU legacy bonds collapsed.

Fortunately, through a combination of a recovery in the capital markets post-Lehman (points 4 and 5), slightly improving earnings (point 6), and good financial engineering (point 5), there was a recovery in the bonds, although they continued to trade at distressed levels.

· WHAT WE KNOW ·

1. It is easier to value a bond than a stock because bonds mature. You will get paid par at maturity, and you will receive semiannual contractual interest payments unless the company defaults.

2. The volatility of price movement is an important aspect of risk.

3. Credit risk is the most important aspect of risk in junk bonds.

CHAPTER 13

DEFAULTS AND JUNK BONDS

The key to performance is minimizing your future default experience; the Strong-Horse Method helps you do that.

When a company defaults, it generally does not die because the U.S. Bankruptcy Code tends to give companies a chance at a new life. Investors in the company, on the other hand, may or may not be wiped out: equity investors in most cases lose their whole investment; senior, secured bank lenders often do not lose any money; and the junk bond investors are left somewhere in between. How much junk bond investors recover depends on many factors that we will not detail in this book. Suffice it to say that it is a bad event if you buy the bonds of a company assuming it will not default and you are wrong. (Sometimes distressed investing experts will buy the bonds at a low price, assuming the bonds will default.) When a company defaults on its bonds, the price can fall 50 or more points from par.

Default risk is the primary risk in junk bond investing, as opposed to interest rate risk for high grade investing. The analysis of default risk is called *corporate credit analysis*. High grade bond analytics, as opposed to junk bond analytics, are different and can be quite quantitative, centering on the relationship between the maturity of the underlying issue and the expected movement of interest rates. This type of quantitative analysis is only of secondary importance to junk bonds as most junk bond new issues have a shorter maturity, 10 years or less, while high grade bonds can go out 30 years (some have a 100-year maturity). Also, the junk bond coupon is so high that it plays a more significant role in expected returns. Finally, when the economy and corporate profits grow, interest rates tend to rise, which is bad for all bonds, but credit rating upgrades can mitigate this erosion in junk bonds.

CAUSES OF FAILURE

There are many causes of junk bond failure. A junk bond issuer could fail because its products become obsolete or uncompetitive or the company could be poorly managed. I have seen healthcare companies fail because of a change in medical reimbursements. I have seen casinos fail because newer, neighboring jurisdictions take customers away or because the casinos have lost their appeal. Auto companies have failed because of poor management. Private equity demands on all their acquisitions place terrible burdens on issuers, and they often fail for those reasons. Sometimes the reasons compound on one another. For example, a private equity transaction could base its debt levels on one expected growth rate, and then the economy turns south harming the business and killing the company.

As mentioned earlier, some corporate acquirers have a history of repeatedly bankrupting their acquisitions by paying too much and when they encounter unexpected adverse business conditions, they lack the financial flexibility to overcome these problems. I call these owners *serial defaulters*. It is important to search the default history of the owners or CEOs of the company in which you invest. Wheeler-dealers, such as entrepreneurs willing to take on enormous amounts of debt in an acquisition, were big factors in the early high yield market of the 1970s, 1980s, and 1990s. Many of those acquisitions ended badly, with lenders losing all their investment. Today, private equity owners are the closest thing to serial defaulters, but, to be fair, in the downturn of 2008, they benefited from weaker deal covenants and came up with innovative features such as *extend-and-amend covenants* to keep companies alive.

Another reason a company could default is its inability to refinance maturing debt and its lack of cash to retire the debt. Hypothetically, a company could forestall default if creditors were willing to provide new loans as debt matures. Unfortunately, this may not happen in the real world. When a company performs poorly, creditors may become unwilling to extend additional loans, forcing the company into default as debt payments are due. There are also times when a company is performing well, but credit is unavailable to the market as a whole. This occurred in 2008 following Lehman Brothers' bankruptcy, when banks were unwilling to lend for their own reasons, and during the end of the Drexel period (late 1980s–early 1990s), when the Federal Reserve prohibited banks from lending to highly leveraged transactions (HLT). Therefore, it is important to consider the debt maturity schedule of any company when investing in its bonds.

Surprisingly, the definition of *default* is hotly contested. Some people view a default as the filings in bankruptcy court. Others, such as the ratings agencies, view it as investors not receiving full principal or interest back in a timely manner. Amending an indenture and paying investors less than what they originally signed on for would be a default to them. This default would include amended deals.

EMERGING FROM DEFAULT

Companies do not always successfully emerge from default. Oftentimes, the business is so bad that it cannot meet its new debt obligations. This situation occurred with Movie Gallery, which filed for Chapter 11 bankruptcy in 2007 the first time and failed to reorganize a second time, resulting in liquidation that year via Chapter 7. Movie Gallery could not keep up with the high debt, declining revenue, and increased costs associated with by-mail competitors such as Netflix and Blockbuster.

Sometimes the company has too much debt both before and after emerging from bankruptcy. Such was the case with Pliant Corp, which began life as Huntsman Packaging. A combination of too much debt, higher than expected costs, and Hurricanes Katrina and Rita triggered the first bankruptcy in 2005. This first bankruptcy pitted secured and unsecured creditors in a ferocious battle, and what emerged was an ill-conceived plan that did not last. Distressed investors got control in the second bankruptcy and sold the company to Berry Plastics. Other multiple defaults were Trump Casinos, which entered bankruptcy three times—1992, 2004, and 2009—and Trico Marine, provider of offshore supply services to oil and gas companies, primarily in the North Sea and the Gulf of Mexico. Trico filed in 2004 and 2010.

CYCLE FREQUENCY

There seems to always be a crisis and then a recovery in the high yield market, and the cycles appear to be occurring with more frequency. We can see this in Figure 13.1, which shows the default history of the "market" since 1986 and the "spread to worst" of the market superimposed for the same time period. Notice the twin peaks of high defaults during the 1989 to 1990 period (when Drexel went bankrupt) and the 2008 to 2009 period (the credit crisis). Generally, periods of high defaults are followed by several years of extremely low defaults, declining spreads, and tremendous opportunity for high returns. Recovery is as strong as the downturn is violent.

Notice, in Figure 13.1, the spread rises (the price falls) prior to companies' defaulting and subsequently recovers strongly. In between were the 1998 collapse of Long-Term Capital Management (LTCM) Hedge Fund, the telecom bub-

Figure 13.1 High Yield Default Rate Versus JPMorgan High Yield Index Spreads

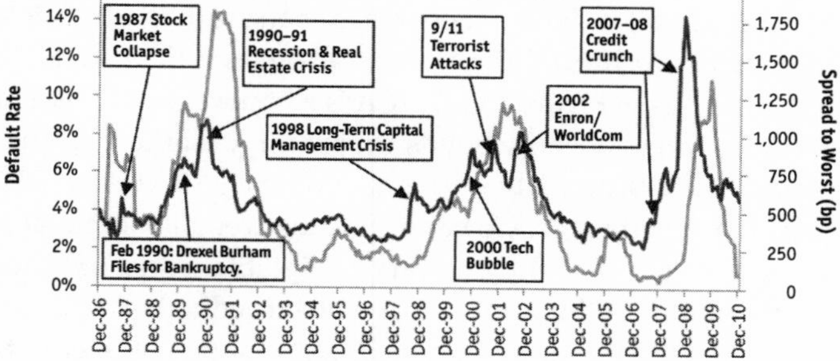

Source: Peter Acciavatti et al., *JPMorgan 2009 High Yield Annual Review.*

Table 13.1 HCA

	2007	2008	2009
Revenue	$26,858	$28,374	$30,052
EBITDA	$4,831	$4,378	$5,093
Leverage	5.6	6.1	4.9
Coverage	2.2	2.2	2.6
Source: Revenue from company disclosures.			

ble bursting in 2001, the terrorist attacks in 2001, the Enron/ WorldCom corporate frauds disclosures, and finally the 2007 to 2008 credit crunch.

A crisis is often a time to invest in Strong-Horse companies. For example, during the worst of the recent recession (November to December 2008), the best BB credits traded in the $70s and the B credits at $50; many CCC-rated credits traded in the $10 to $20 price range. This was an extraordinary time to invest in high quality companies at good prices. One such company was the hospital management corporation HCA, which was a darling of Wall Street for many years. It was taken private in 2006 for $31.6 billion by a consortium of KKR, Bain, Merrill Lynch, and the Frist family (the founders). The revenue, EBITDA, leverage, and coverage are shown in Table 13.1.

The second-priority senior secured 9.25% due 2016 bonds rated BB– by Standard & Poor's dropped from $105 to $73, subsequently recovered throughout 2009, and then traded at $109 in 2011 (see Figure 13.2). HCA is a noncyclical, recession-resistant company whose bonds dropped for market technical reasons. In 2008, notice that revenues rose by 5.5% and EBITDA declined by nearly 10%. However, coverage remained the same, leverage increased slightly, to very acceptable levels, but most important, the outlook for 2009 was exceedingly bright. An investment at $78 would result in a 9.25% coupon plus a capital gain to the current trading price (between $105 and $110).

Figure 13.2 HCA 9.25% Due 2016 Bond Price

Source: JP Morgan. Used by permission.

Another example of investing in a good credit whose price declined for technical or liquidity reasons, and not for credit reasons, comes from a company located in my state of New Jersey: NRG Energy is a BB--rated power generation company with plants located domestically and internationally. Notice in Table 13.2 and Figure 13.3 how the NRG bond traded similarly to

Figure 13.3 NRG 7.375% Due 2016 Bond Price

Source: JP Morgan. Used by permission.

Table 13.2 NRG Energy

	2007	2008	2009
Revenue	$5,989	$6,885	$8,952
EBITDA	$2,310	$3,170	3,122
Leverage	3.4X	2.4X	2.5X
Coverage	3.3X	5.4X	4.9X
Source: Revenue from company disclosures.			

Table 13.3   Default Rate Comparison*

YEAR	JP MORGAN	STRONG HORSE
1991	11.5%	0.00%
1992	4.4%	0.00%
1993	2.3%	0.00%
1994	1.4%	0.00%
1995	2.8%	0.00%
1996	1.6%	0.00%
1997	1.4%	0.00%
1998	1.7%	0.00%
1999	4.0%	0.00%
2000	4.9%	0.00%
2001	8.6%	2.09%
2002	7.5%	0.00%
2003	3.1%	0.99%
2004	1.1%	0.00%
2005	2.7%	0.11%
2006	0.9%	0.07%
2007	0.4%	0.00%
2008	2.2%	0.96%
2009	10.3%	7.95%
2010	0.8%	n/a

*Default Rate Statistics of the High Yield Market Based on the JPMorgan High Yield Index Compared with the Strong-Horse Investing Statistics

Sources: JPMorgan Default Monitor and Nomura Corporate Research and Asset Management, High Yield Total Return Institutional Composite (HYTRIC). Used by permission.

HCA's 9.25% issue. Even with solid ratios and margins through 2007 and 2008, the bond still dropped sharply to a low of $73, but it was able to recoup those losses by the end of 2009. An investment at the trough would generate a 7.375% coupon plus the capital gain to the trading range between $105 and $110.

Avoiding defaults is a great way to make money in the junk bond market—that is what I did. Table 13.3 shows the default statistics of the high yield market based on the JPMorgan High Yield Default Monitor compared with the Strong-Horse Investing statistics. This comparison is presented in Figure 13.4. While Strong-Horse defaults were markedly lower than the market, I was able to sell bonds (often at a loss), while the market index cannot do this, making the comparison not exact.

Figure 13.4 Default Rate Statistics of the High Yield Market Based on the JPMorgan High Yield Index Compared with the Strong-Horse Investing Statistics

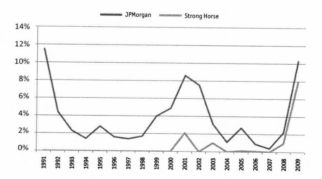

Sources: JPMorgan Default Monitor and Nomura Corporate Research and Asset Management, High Yield Total Return Institutional Composite (HYTRIC). Used by permission.

• WHAT WE KNOW •

1. The biggest risk in junk bond investing is default risk. Your goal is to minimize this risk by using the Strong-Horse Method of credit analysis.

2. There are many reasons a company can default; the two most common are high business risk and high financial risk. Also important is the ability of a company to refinance debt coming due.

3. There's always a cycle when prices fall. If you have good credit analysis skills, however, a crisis is a time to make money by investing in companies whose bond prices have fallen too much.

CHAPTER 14

TESTS THAT SHOW THE STRONG-HORSE METHOD WORKS

We saw in Chapter 4 that the Strong-Horse Method outperformed both the equities (S&P 500) and the high yield market. Here are more details confirming the method's performance and more reasons why it is worth taking the time to learn about it.

Let's start with a simple comparison of the results of Strong-Horse Investing over the period I founded and was running the high yield asset management business at Nomura. Figures 14.1 and 14.2 show the results. Between October 1991 and March 2010, the Strong-Horse Method returned nearly 700%, while the high yield market as measured by the BoA Merrill Lynch Index returned 350% and the S&P 500 stock index returned 325%. On an average annual return basis, this translates into nearly a 12% return compared to the junk bond market return of 8.7% and slightly less than that for the stock market (S&P 500 Index) at 8.1%. The numbers are compelling!

Figure 14.1 Average Annualized Return Since Inception of the Strong-Horse Method, October 1, 1991, to March 31, 2010

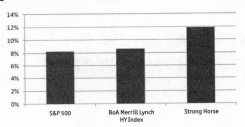

Sources: BoA Merrill Lynch High Yield Bond Indices and Nomura Corporate Research and Asset Management, High Yield Total Return Institutional Composite (HYTRIC). Used by permission.

Figure 14.2 Cumulative Return Since Inception of the Strong-Horse Method, October 1, 1991, to March 31, 2010

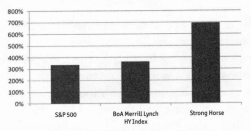

Sources: BoA Merrill Lynch High Yield Bond Indices and Nomura Corporate Research and Asset Management, High Yield Total Return Institutional Composite (HYTRIC). Used by permission.

Be warned, the system does not work every quarter or every year. But as I've said, there is generally a crisis in both the capital markets and the junk bond market every few years. Those periods of crisis can be terrific times to invest. Remember that you are lending to companies, not to the market. In addition, the market has always come back because the strong companies repay their debts and meet their interest payments. The default rate can go up, but we will avoid most of those defaults by finding companies that will repay their obligations.

In fact, the best time to apply the Strong-Horse Method is after the market falls. The market reflects many things: the economic outlook, new trends, new technologies, new financial engineering, and other changes in the world around us. For example, the junk bond market could fall because the stock market had a selloff due to an anticipated Greek, Irish, or Portuguese failure. Or there could be fear that a banking crisis could bring down the financial system. I would rather buy the bonds of a Strong-Horse company at 60 or 70 cents on the dollar than 100 cents or 110 cents on the dollar, all else being equal.

Figure 14.1 compares the average annualized return of the S&P 500 Index, BoA Merrill Lynch High Yield Index, and Strong-Horse Method since October 1, 1991—inception of the Strong-Horse Method—through March 31, 2010. This graph shows the average return per year each strategy would yield for the time frame. Notice how the Strong-Horse Method's return is nearly 12%, while the S&P 500 and the BoA Merrill Lynch High Yield Index both return less than 9%.

Figure 14.2 compares the cumulative returns of the three investment strategies since inception of the Strong-Horse Method. Thus $1,000 invested on October 1, 1991, would be worth about $8,000 using the Strong-Horse Method, while it would be worth only about $3,600 and $3,400 with the BoA Merrill Lynch High Yield Index and S&P 500 Index, respectively.

An 18½-year track record is good, but the devil is in the details. If in 1991 and 1992 we entered the market when it was "cheap" and in 2010 the market was "rich" and we lost money for all years in between, that would not be a good strategy. Actually we did enter the market when it was cheap in 1991 and left when it was up a lot in 2010. Those of you who understand numbers know that the end points of a multiyear comparison dominate the results. We have to look at shorter and intermediate time frames in order to see how we performed. I'll refresh a table we looked at earlier (Table 14.1).

Table 14.1 Annualized Comparable Returns Since Inception of the Strong-Horse Method, October 1, 1991, to March 31, 2010

RETURN	S&P 500	BoA MERRILL LYNCH HY INDEX	STRONG HORSE
1 yr	49.8%	57.0%	64.5%
5 yr	1.9%	7.7%	8.2%
10 yr	−0.7%	7.6%	9.4%
15 yr	7.8%	7.7%	10.3%
18½ yr	8.3%	8.7%	11.9%

Sources: BoA Merrill Lynch High Yield Bond Indices and Nomura Corporate Research and Asset Management, High Yield Total Return Institutional Composite (HYTRIC). Used by permission.

We looked at 1-, 5-, 10-, and 15-year time periods ending March 31, 2010, and the period since inception of the Strong-Horse Method. In each of those time periods, the Strong-Horse Method of selecting junk bonds outperformed both the BoA Merrill Lynch High Yield Index and the S&P 500 Index. The 1-year return is so large for all three that it requires some comment.

The year 2008 was a dramatic year in the capital markets. The financial center of the United States nearly collapsed. In particular, the banking sector was in the emergency room. As a result, the various markets crashed. As prices spiraled down, many institutional investors (such as pension funds, mutual funds, or professional money managers) tried to liquidate their investments. There was more selling pressure than buying demand, which fueled the decline in prices. In the high yield market, we had the paradox that the best credits fell in price more than the worst credits because only the best credits could be sold and traded. The pricing service reflected those actual transactions and accepted the brokerage firms' estimates for untraded bonds, and thus only the best credits were marked down to actual transaction prices. The weaker or illiquid credits were never marked down to their fair market value by the pricing services. Their prices were only guesswork because no transactions of these credits were taking place. In 2009, when the economic outlook improved, prices rebounded, and thus you see the outsized returns that year.

The story above cries out for more performance detail. How did the Strong-Horse Method perform in 2007 and 2008 when the market crashed? Not well. You can see this poor performance in Table 14.2, which shows the annual performance since we started managing money in 1991.

The Strong-Horse Method does not work every quarter or every year or two. However, it works over a long time period, as long as you invest in undervalued companies that meet our credit criteria.

The Strong-Horse Method underperformed the high yield market in 2008 (it outperformed the stock market, based on the S&P 500). Remember, bonds that do not default pay par at maturity. The bond market recovery in 2009 was spectacular. The government provided stability to the banking sector (remember "Too Big to Fail"). Multiple new issues of the best credits were priced at several percentage points (hundreds of basis points) more than they should have been. Other bond managers saw the tempting yields for the best junk credits and jumped on the bandwagon. First, the highest quality issues were bought, and finally, when the recovery was more evident, the lowest quality issues were bought. The CCC sector return was greater than 100% that year.

Table 14.2 Annual Comparable Returns Since Inception of the Strong-Horse Method, October 1, 1991, to March 31, 2010

RETURN	S&P 500	BoA MERRILL LYNCH HY INDEX	STRONG HORSE
Q4 1991	8.0%	5.4%	4.4%
1992	7.6%	18.2%	19.3%
1993	10.1%	17.2%	26.0%
1994	1.3%	−1.2%	9.4%
1995	37.6%	19.9%	23.7%
1996	23.0%	11.1%	20.8%
1997	33.4%	12.8%	20.5%
1998	28.6%	3.7%	0.2%
1999	21.0%	1.6%	7.5%
2000	−9.1%	−3.8%	−5.1%
2001	−11.9%	6.2%	15.0%
2002	−22.1%	−1.1%	4.7%
2003	28.7%	27.2%	26.9%
2004	10.9%	10.8%	12.7%
2005	4.9%	2.8%	3.5%
2006	15.8%	10.8%	13.1%
2007	5.5%	2.5%	1.6%
2008	−37.0%	−26.1%	−29.5%
2009	26.5%	58.1%	64.4%
Q1 2010	5.4%	4.8%	6.1%

Sources: BoA Merrill Lynch High Yield Bond Indices and Nomura Corporate Research and Asset Management, High Yield Total Return Institutional Composite (HYTRIC). Used by permission.

· WHAT WE KNOW ·

1. The Strong-Horse track record outperformed both the S&P 500 Index and the BoA Merrill Lynch High Yield Index for the 1-, 5-, 10-, 15-, and 18½-year periods.

2. The method does not work every quarter or every year, but over many years, it provides above average returns.

MORE STATISTICAL TESTS

I am a New York Yankees fan. I know that in certain places it is dangerous to admit that fact. When I was a youngster living in a low-income housing project in New York City, a famous social service agency, the Henry Street Settlement, used to take street urchins such as my friends and me to New York Yankees baseball games at the old stadium, built in 1923—The House That Ruth Built. It was as much fun to sneak into the box seats from the bleachers as it was to watch the game. When you are small, there are numerous ways to get out of the bleachers. We would squeeze between the bars, under the bars, or find a hole in the dilapidated concrete.

Let's talk baseball. What does baseball have to do with junk bonds? Not a whole lot besides the fact that Citigroup, the financial services company that bought the naming rights to the New York Mets' new stadium, trades them. Another thing junk bonds—and all financial instruments for that matter—have in common with baseball is statistics. Everything in baseball, as in finance, is quantified. Fans want to know who are the best pitchers, batters, and shortstops in the league. While "the best" is highly subjective and just as highly debatable, we analyze statistics to help make our arguments. One common statistic used in baseball is the batting average: the ratio of hits to at bats.

BATTING AVERAGES

Batting average is an important statistic. If a player batted only once and got a hit, he would be batting 1,000. If he hit once after batting twice, he would be batting 500. One hit out of three and he would now be batting 333. Got it? It's important to understand the statistics that you're dealing with. For example, let's say a batter has two hits, a groundout, and a walk. What would his batting average be? It would be 667 because a walk does not count as a hit *or* an at bat. That is why there is another statistic called *on-base percentage*. The averages are kept throughout the entire season, and at the end of the season, fans can see who the best hitters in the league are statistically.

How has the Strong-Horse Method performed over the past 20 or so years? The truth is in the numbers. I could tell you that the Strong-Horse Method *outperformed* the high yield market and the S&P 500 Index 68% and 60% of the time, respectively, over the past 10 years. I could also tell you that the Strong-Horse Method slightly *outperformed* the S&P 500 over the past 10 years annualized with only about half the volatility, but that fact still may not convince you. Annualized data do not always paint the complete picture and can sometimes be misleading. There must be a better way to illustrate the Strong-Horse Method's performance.

This same idea can be applied to financial performance. To make comparisons simpler, the fiscal year is broken down into quarters. Let's say each quarter is an at bat, and each time the Strong-Horse Method beats the BoA Merrill Lynch High Yield Index, that can be considered a hit. So, in one year, if the Strong-Horse Method beats the BoA Merrill Lynch HY Index twice, and it loses twice, it would also have a batting average of 500 (50.0%). Let's see in Figures 15.1 through 15.3 how the Strong-Horse Method has actually fared over the past 18½ years.

Figure 15.1 Five-Year Batting Average, Second Quarter 2005 Through First Quarter 2010

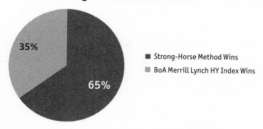

Sources: BoA Merrill Lynch High Yield Bond Indices and Nomura Corporate Research and Asset Management, High Yield Total Return Institutional Composite (HYTRIC). Used by permission.

Figure 15.2 Ten-Year Batting Average, Second Quarter 2000 Through First Quarter 2010

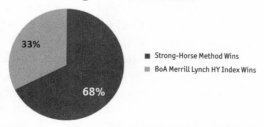

Sources: BoA Merrill Lynch High Yield Bond Indices and Nomura Corporate Research and Asset Management, High Yield Total Return Institutional Composite (HYTRIC). Used by permission.

Figure 15.3 Batting Average Since Inception of Strong-Horse
Method, Fourth Quarter 1991 Through First Quarter 2010

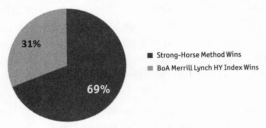

- Strong-Horse Method Wins
- BoA Merrill Lynch HY Index Wins

Sources: BoA Merrill Lynch High Yield Bond Indices and Nomura Corporate Research and Asset
Management, High Yield Total Return Institutional Composite (HYTRIC). Used by permission.

The results are nearly identical for the three time periods.
In fact, the Strong-Horse Method actually improves as the time
horizon increases. Therefore, the method is not only effective
but also consistent.

RISKS AND RETURNS

Return is important but risk measurement is too. The risk in
junk bonds is primarily credit risk: the assessment of a company's ability to avoid a payment default. There is also the risk of
the entire asset class. Is the return of the asset class sufficient to
make an investment in these risky securities? There have been
numerous studies over the past 30 years.[1] Also, many "risk managers" have studied the high yield sector and positioned the risk
of junk bonds relative to many other asset classes.

One common measure is the amount of money you can
lose in an investment relative to the amount of money you can
earn. Another measure is the volatility of the returns. The second measure is generally accepted in the investment world,

but it requires some additional explanation (see Chapter 12, "Bond Price Volatility"). Therefore, we must consider both risk and return when determining the "best" investment strategy. Luckily, a Nobel Prize–winning economist by the name of William Forsyth Sharpe invented a formula that can combine these two metrics: the Sharpe ratio. The Sharpe ratio calculates the return per unit of risk. Now we can see which method generated the best return for each unit of risk taken (Table 15.1).

Table 15.1 Sharpe Ratio Comparison

RETURN	S&P 500	BoA MERRILL LYNCH HY INDEX	STRONG HORSE
1 yr	3.73	5.19	5.76
5 yr	0.12	0.58	0.58
10 yr	−0.04	0.69	0.81
15 yr	0.49	0.82	0.99
18½ yr	0.56	1.01	1.24

Sources: Calculations based on data provided by BoA Merrill Lynch High Yield Bond Indices and Nomura Corporate Research and Asset Management, High Yield Total Return Institutional Composite (HYTRIC). Used by permission.

The formula for the Sharpe ratio is as follows:

$$S = \frac{R_p - \text{RFR}}{\sigma}$$

In other words, the Sharpe ratio (S) is the average return of a representative portfolio (R_p) minus the average risk-free assets return (RFR), all divided by the standard deviation of the representative portfolio. All measures are for the same time period.

Typically the risk-free rate used is the three-month Treasury bill. At the time of this writing, the three-month Treasury bill interest rate is 0.16% and the inflation rate is 0.15%. Therefore, we will assume the risk-free rate is zero for the purposes of this book.

The Strong-Horse Method of investing in junk bonds has offered at least as much and often more return per unit of risk than either the stock market (as represented by the S&P 500 Index) and the high yield market (as measured by the BoA Merrill Lynch High Yield Index) in all the periods measured in Table 15.1—that is, in the 1-, 5-, 10-, 15-, and 18½-year periods ending March 31, 2010. Also, the BoA Merrill Lynch High Yield Index Sharpe ratio was superior to the S&P 500 Index in all the respective periods. One reason is that equity volatility is greater than high yield volatility.

A typical investment chart would look as follows: return on one axis and risk (volatility) on the other. Figure 15.4 is a comparison of different asset classes.

Figure 15.4 Risk Versus Return

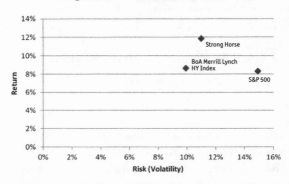

Note: Annualized volatility calculated based on monthly returns for 18½ years ending March 31, 2010.

Sources: BoA Merrill Lynch High Yield Bond Indices and Nomura Corporate Research and Asset Management, High Yield Total Return Institutional Composite (HYTRIC). Used by permission.

· WHAT WE KNOW ·

1. The "batting average," while not a standard measure of investment performance, is an interesting and informative statistic to use when assessing investment performance.

2. The use of different time frames enhances this performance comparison.

3. Return measures tell only part of the story; return per unit of risk is useful as well.

4. By any measure, the New York Yankees have had a storied history.

CHAPTER 16

How to Invest in Junk Bonds: Logistics

In 2000, the SEC adopted Regulation FD for the purpose of evening out the dissemination of information by companies to the investment community. The theory was that all investors, individuals, and institutions should have equal access to company information. In my opinion, despite Regulation FD, the institutional investor for both stocks and bonds has an advantage over the retail investor. If you plan to purchase individual credits, let me again caution you about the risks and disadvantages of doing so:

- With most brokers, there is a disadvantage to buying *odd lots*—small amounts—in that you most likely will pay more than if you bought a *round lot* (250 bonds). However, during a recent discussion I had with an odd lot trader at a major securities firm, he insisted his prices were the same as institutional prices, and he further explained that investors could see on the TRACE system the transaction prices for all sizes of trades.

- There is an information imbalance between institutional and individual traders: high quality information is more accessible to institutional traders. They are equipped with the tools and resources to obtain this information more quickly and easily. Large institutional buyers (for example, mutual or pension funds) typically have dozens of different brokers calling or e-mailing investment ideas on a daily basis, with their research departments following up. They also have expensive, sophisticated trading platforms that provide better, faster, and more current pricing information.

- Many bonds are traded privately, meaning that these issues are not registered with the SEC. In order to trade these private (unregistered) bonds, one must be an institutional investor with a certain amount of investable assets. Most junk bonds initially are sold privately and subsequently become public. Individuals are thus closed out of the new issue junk bond market. However, there are many publicly registered junk bonds—enough for a private individual to create a portfolio.

- Diversification is key. You need a lot of capital to create a bond portfolio, and most investors don't have that amount available. For example, if you own only 5 different credits of the same size, 20% of your investment is in the hands of a single speculative grade company if it defaults. If you own 10 credits and one of them defaults, 10% of your portfolio defaults. This situation is diagrammed in Figure 16.1. Therefore, I recommend having *at least* 20 different credits for proper diversification—meaning that only 5% is at risk per holding. With odd lot purchases, one still can create a portfolio.

Figure 16.1 Diversification Curve

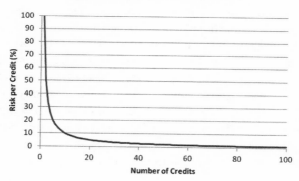

Despite the above risks, a diligent investor can select enough public bonds to purchase a portfolio successfully.

Figure 16.1 shows that as you diversify—buy more unique credits—your risk per credit lessens. This effect is dramatic for the first 20 credits and becomes marginal after that. However, 20 unique credits is the *minimum* I recommend for a properly diversified portfolio.

As a reminder, in order to view a list of registered junk bonds, start with the FINRA Market Data Center website. Once again, here's how:

1. Google "FINRA bond prices" to find the website.

2. Select "Advanced Bond Search" in the Quick Bond Search box.

3. Select "Corporate" as bond type.

4. Enter the criteria you wish to screen (for example, select the Standard & Poor's rating range of BB+ to CCC−).

5. Select "Show Results."

Once you have your criteria screened, you can sort the results by yield, price, or some other characteristic. Clicking on an individual issue will give you specific information such as call price and date, trade activity, and a price chart. The FINRA website provides a wealth of information: prices, yields, rankings, and other current data, along with a list of the most actively traded bonds.

Next, do your homework. After you've found a company you're interested in, go to the SEC website and check out the company's financials and other primary documents. Every mandatory SEC filing can be found on its website:

1. Go to www.sec.gov. Private companies often provide their financials on their corporate website through a link to their SEC filings. For example, in the case of Berry Plastics, we had to go to its corporate website in order to find its SEC filing more easily. In addition, because of Regulation FD, when companies make analyst presentations, they have to provide that presentation to the SEC website as current information.

2. Select "Search for Company Filings" under the Filings and Forms section header.

3. Select "Company or Fund Name . . ." for search method.

4. Enter the company name (for example, "Solo Cup").

5. From the search results, select your desired company.

6. See the list of filings. We often use the 10-K (annual report), 10-Q (quarterly report), and some 8-Ks (special filings such as company presentations).

The final step is to set up a brokerage account. There are online, discount, regional, and national brokerage firms. Find one that suits your needs and charges commissions and fees you are satisfied with. (Note that we use only the free, publicly available information to perform a Strong-Horse analysis in this book.)

· WHAT WE KNOW ·

1. The institutional investor has an advantage over the individual investor in both stocks and bonds.

2. For those investors interested in purchasing junk bonds themselves, there are some caveats, which are listed above.

3. There is enough disclosure and price information to accumulate a portfolio of odd lot purchases.

CHAPTER 17

COVENANTS

Management is a fiduciary to shareholders, not bondholders. The only legal protection a bondholder has against adverse corporate or outside actions is the contract between the company and the bondholder. That contract is called an *indenture.* Within the indenture is a list of agreements called *covenants* that are extraordinarily important. Covenants spell out the rights and protections afforded bondholders. Management can talk to bondholders, smile a lot and be pleasant, especially when they want your money. However, management does not work for the bondholder; the only protection is in the indenture. And in degree of difficulty, reading the indenture is second only to reading the tax code.

As I've said before, the devil is in the details. Imagine you, or even the institutional investor, reading the indenture or the prospectus. Those documents are drafted by a team of high-priced lawyers working for the issuer (the company). Most often in private equity deals, the owners have a team of highly compensated professionals crafting one-sided documents by the best and brightest corporate lawyers in accordance with their client's demands. These documents are then reviewed by an investment banking team of financiers to see how far they can push the envelope even further in favor of their client. An army of costly advisors reviews the indenture and then have discussions with rating agencies before the finished product is delivered to potential bond buyers. The situation is similar to a basketball game with five people against one, the investor being the one. Sometimes the buyers have read the indenture, but oftentimes they are not given a chance. For example, a *drive-by financing* is one in which the issuer provides no documentation to the buyer prior to the purchase—this often happens in a "hot" market.

I have provided this level of description to point out that the relationship is one-sided when it comes to covenants—and that side is against the bond buyer. Many institutional buyers seek out help in analyzing covenants. One company, Covenant Review, is often used for new financings. That being said, I will give you a list of covenants to look for. Be warned, however, that a bond issuer can seem to provide that covenant while simultaneously negating its effectiveness with a craftily drafted sentence or paragraph embedded in the covenant description. I have seen covenants that appeared good, but after five pages of definitions and qualifiers, the last sentence would read, "This covenant will not apply if . . ." The "if," not surprisingly, happens.

Paradoxically, junk issuers have better covenants than investment grade issuers. The size of the losses by investment grade bond buyers can be staggering when a seemingly great company (perhaps rated AA) is taken over by a private equity buyer and the bonds drop to a CCC rating.

Below is a list of several of the most important covenants:

Key Covenants

- Disclosure

- Change of control

- Call features

- Debt incurrence

- Restricted payments

- Security

- Maintenance of a credit rating level

Let's take a closer look at each one.

DISCLOSURE

One year after an initial public offering, public companies do not have to file their subsequent financial performance publicly to the SEC if they have fewer than 500 holders of their securities. Many companies prefer not to disclose publicly to the SEC, claiming it is expensive. Investors and Wall Street traders need the disclosure for trading purposes. Lack of disclosure is a huge impediment to establishing an active market to buy and sell junk bonds as issuers typically have fewer than 500 holders, and thus they do not have to disclose their financials publicly. At one time, this issue was huge, but after a concentrated bondholder effort, companies were forced to disclose to the

SEC. However, companies are still trying to figure out how to get around this covenant.

CHANGE OF CONTROL

Let's say you want to lend to Company A because it is well capitalized (it has little debt), it is run by a management team you respect, and it is publicly owned with a wide cross-section of owners. Also, your bonds could be rated A or BBB. Along comes Mr. Private Equity, who convinces the board of directors that his offer to buy the company is superior to the market price and then takes over the company. The new company now is poorly capitalized with tons of debt, and, surprise, your debt is junior in the capital structure to all other debt. The company's rating has dropped to CCC– and trades at 50 cents on the dollar. This used to happen often until junk bond investors insisted on the *change-of-control covenant*. Simply stated, this covenant allows holders to put back (sell) their bonds to the issuer at a $101 price in the event of a change of control such as a takeover.

For most deals, this covenant works the way it was intended; however, sometimes it is crafted to appear real, but it is actually watered down so much as to be worthless. Sometimes the covenant is wholly disingenuous. This case occurred with the Apollo takeover of AMC (the movie theater company). Apollo controlled AMC in 2004 and arranged a sale to JPMorgan Partners and a different Apollo fund. A multipage change-of-control covenant was written so that this sale would not trigger a change of control for bondholders but *did* trigger the covenant for the preferred stock Apollo owned. In my opinion this action did not follow the spirit of the covenant. More important, it shows the one-sided nature of the relationship between private equity and the bondholders on which they rely.

Call Features

Most high yield bonds give the issuer the option of *calling back the bonds* according to a set schedule. The issuer pays a price called the *call premium* for this option. For example, a typical 10-year bond would be noncallable for 5 years and callable starting after the end of the noncall period. The premium usually starts at half the coupon and declines to zero premium at maturity. Recently, companies have tried to change the call dates and call premiums to make it more advantageous to issuers to call their bonds cheaply.

Debt Incurrence and Restricted Payments

These are two of the most important financial covenants protecting bond investors. *Debt incurrence* limits the amount of debt a company can take on, and *restricted payments* limits the amount of dividends and other types of payments a company can make. Taken together, these covenants place some restrictions on acquirers' borrowing too much money and paying themselves a huge dividend with the proceeds. When these covenants are too loose, as frequently happens, there can be disastrous consequences.

A typical debt incurrence test would limit borrowings up to (1) a fixed charge coverage ratio not to go below an acceptable level, (2) a dollar amount, and (3) sometimes a percentage of tangible equity. For example, the Owens-Illinois debt issue previously used (7.38% of 2016) limits new debt to a 2:1 fixed charge coverage and limits borrowings to a certain dollar maximum and a percentage of tangible equity. A typical restricted payments test would limit corporate money used for dividends or any distribution (cash or otherwise), stock repurchases, or repurchases of debt subordinated to the debt you hold. All of these actions would not be permitted unless, after giving effect to the distributions, the company can borrow $1. That is, satisfying the *debt incurrence test*. Also, some tests include a limitation that a percent of the net income (say, 50%) be retained by the business.

Unfortunately, these covenants are not drafted as clearly as stated above. Also, there are often pages of exceptions and clarifications. Investing in junk bonds can be easy, but unfortunately, covenant analysis requires a lot of work.

Security

A *secured bondholder* has a huge advantage over unsecured bondholders in the event of bankruptcy. Secured bondholders have to be made whole before unsecured bondholders can receive anything. For that reason, secured debt is less risky than unsecured debt. Such debt also yields less than unsecured debt and for most companies provides a lower return than unsecured debt. Bank loans, for example, are secured, and over the past several years, they were offered to institutional junk bond buyers. There are levels of security such as first lien debt and second lien debt. In the late 1980s and early 1990s, foreign buyers wanted to buy only secured debt. Drexel Burnham crafted indentures to satisfy these buyers by offering first-priority secured debt, second-priority secured debt, third-priority secured debt, and so on. They took advantage of unsophisticated buyers by essentially taking unsecured debt and repackaging it as secured debt far down the security chain of a capital structure.

MAINTENANCE OF CREDIT RATING LEVEL

Sometimes, when a debt deal is difficult, covenants are added to appease the buyer. One such deal was done by The Gap, Inc. The 8.8% bonds due December 15, 2008, were issued on November 16, 2001, and they were rated Baa2/BBB+ by Moody's and Standard & Poor's. There was a covenant that required a coupon increase or decrease of 25 basis points for each upgrade or downgrade by Moody's or Standard & Poor's. The coupon would be reset every June 15 and December 15 if there were any upgrades or downgrades. The bonds were subsequently downgraded by Moody's to Baa3 on January 14, 2002, Ba2 on February 14, 2002, and Ba3 on February 27, 2002, a four-notch total since the time of the new issue. The coupon was also downgraded three notches by Standard & Poor's. Therefore, on June 15, 2002, the coupon on the bonds increased to 10.55% (25 bp times the 7-notch downgrade). Needless to say, the bond price went up with each downgrade. This situation was highly unusual, and as a bondholder, I loved every downgrade!

· WHAT WE KNOW ·

1. Covenants are a key bondholder protection. While there are many, I suggest focusing on the covenants described in the chapter.

2. The key covenants are these:

- Disclosure
- Change of control
- Call features
- Debt incurrence
- Restricted payments
- Security
- Maintenance of a credit rating level

CHAPTER 18

THE GOOD, THE UGLY, AND THE BAD

One of my favorite old movies is a western called *The Good, the Bad, and the Ugly*, released in the mid-1960s. The movie centered on three characters—all less than ideal citizens intent on killing each other and anyone who got in their way in finding a buried treasure. While none of the three were law-abiding, the Clint Eastwood character—"the Good"—appeals to people through charisma and charm. He is able to overcome various trials and tribulations and succeed in achieving his goal. In contrast is Lee Van Cleef—"the Bad"—a mean, sociopathic killer with no redeeming features. In between is Eli Wallach—"the Ugly"—a dangerous but comical character whom you wouldn't take home to meet the family but who provides value to the movie.

The original Italian translation was *The Good, the Ugly, and the Bad*, and that is how I characterize junk bonds, in successively declining quality. None of the three rises to the exalted investment grade status. All of these companies are character-ized by a higher debt burden relative to their business model. But you can distinguish their features according to the relation-ship between business risk and financial risk to help you under-stand the differences between the good, ugly, and bad. I do not promise any buried treasure, killings, or other nefarious esca-pades, but thinking about the classes of bonds this way can help you understand the various features.

Good junk bonds have many desirable Strong-Horse fea-tures. They are issued by large, industry-leading companies with a leading market share, positive trends, low cost structure, pricing flexibility, a good balance sheet, and plenty of excess cash flow. In addition, the management team has a history of dealing fairly with bondholders. Finally, the issue has good cov-enants. Typically, an investment in such a company will gen-erate the expected interest and principal. Unfortunately, these bonds do not yield very much. However, they provide a solid long-term return.

What I call "ugly" junk bonds are typically not Strong-Horse investments. They have problems. They could be good businesses with too much debt, or they could be suspect busi-nesses with a reasonable balance sheet. They could have a strategy to survive, and they could be a reasonable speculative investment if the purchase price and risk were low enough.

"Bad" bonds should be avoided. The business trend for these bonds is negative, the leverage is too high, and the busi-ness could fail no matter how much debt there is. When they default, the recovery could be negligible or nonexistent.

The following two chapters discuss these junk bond classes. First we will look at "good" bonds and how to make money investing in them. I like to say that good things happen to good companies. Next we will look at "ugly" bonds, which can generate above average returns under certain circumstances. Last, we will review "bad" bonds.

· WHAT WE KNOW ·

1. Good junk bonds are the safest and, in many ways, the most desirable.

2. Ugly junk bonds could be a reasonable speculative investment if the purchase price and risk are low enough.

3. Avoid the bad junk bonds.

CHAPTER 19

THE GOOD: GOOD THINGS HAPPEN TO GOOD COMPANIES

This topic is a fun one. Good companies are a pleasure to deal with. They have a solid business, sound financials, a positive outlook, and honorable management. Often, they are market share leaders, have their costs under control as evidenced by high profit margins, and generate excess cash flow. Sometimes, however, these companies may not be yielding enough to excite aggressive buyers. Yet in many cases they are still a good investment.

The junk bond advantage is a high interest rate over a long period of time. Good companies pay their interest on time. In addition, good companies can provide more than par due to the positive credit events discussed in this chapter.

ACHIEVING CAPITAL GAINS

While most people do not think about capital gains in conjunction with junk bonds, there are five positive events that could result in receiving bond prices greater than par: upgrades, change in status to rising star, equity offering, called debt, and tendered debt. Table 19.1 breaks down these events in 2010 to show how gains can be achieved. There were over half a *trillion* dollars of bonds impacted by positive events in 2010.

Table 19.1 Positive Events Impact on Junk Bonds for
the First 11 Months of 2010

Action	Billions of Dollars	Notes
Upgades	$355	Energy-dominated companies
Rising Stars	33	Healthcare; paper and packaging
Equity Offerings	44	28% of all public equity in 2010
Called Debt	61	
Tendered Debt	61	
Total	$554	

Source: Data from *JPMorgan 2010 High Yield Annual Review*.

Upgrades

Improved corporate performance by corporate debt issuers generally results in higher market prices and sometimes upgrades by rating agencies. These upgrades can reduce a company's future interest expense. Sometimes the bond price trades higher with the recognition that the company is a stronger credit with a lower risk of a future default. Often, the companies will call their old debt at a premium and replace it with a new debt issue at a lower coupon (cost). The amounts are not trivial: there were 387 issues upgraded affecting $365 billion of debt in 2010.[1]

Rising Stars

Sometimes rating increases will move companies from junk status to investment grade status. Those companies are called *rising stars*. Because of the high-risk nature of junk bonds, many institutional buyers have restrictions on the amount (if any) of junk bonds they can own. As a result, there is a huge price increase when a junk credit turns into an investment grade credit. There were $33 billion of rising star upgrades in the first 11 months of 2010. Two examples of rising stars are Freeport-McMoRan (FCX) and DirecTV. Both companies have a long history of success. They have accessed the junk bond market numerous times and used the proceeds to build successful businesses.

Freeport-McMoRan, an international copper and gold mining company, has a history of making huge, debt-financed acquisitions and paying down debt over time. It has certainly benefited from the run up of gold and copper prices. The com-

Figure 19.1 Freeport-McMoRan 8.38% Due 2017 Bond Price

Source: JP Morgan. Used by permission.

pany was upgraded by Standard & Poor's in 2008 to BBB and by Moody's in 2010. Its 8.38% due 2017 bonds went from 100 to 110 (Figure 19.1). With sales of almost $19 billion in 2010, Freeport's revenue has been relatively steady over the past four years; however, its EBITDA has increased at an impressive rate.

Figure 19.2 DirecTV 7.625% Due 2016 Bond Price

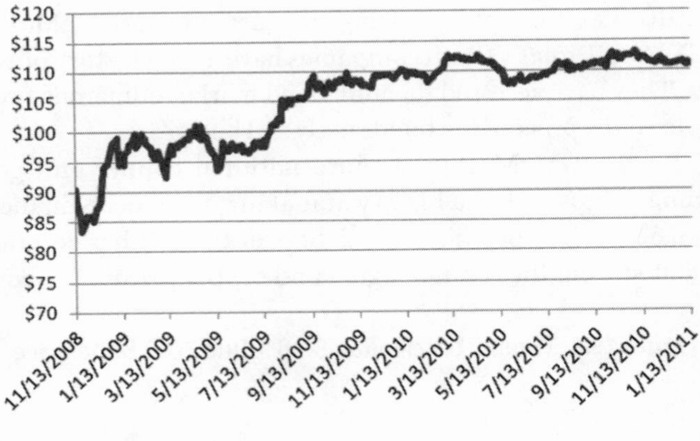

Source: JP Morgan. Used by permission.

DirecTV, a satellite television competitor of cable TV, was upgraded to BBB in early 2010. After the upgrade, the 7.625% due 2016 bonds jumped from 108 to 112 (Figure 19.2). Before the upgrade, the bonds were trading around the 6.5% level; subsequently, the company was able to issue bonds at 5.20%. DirecTV's sales—$21.6 billion in 2009—have grown steadily over the past few years, along with its earnings.

Equity Offers

When a junk bond company issues equity and uses the money for business purposes, either for debt repayment or cash flow enhancement, the champagne tends to flow. Generally, the bond price rises a lot—it is a great day. The company's balance sheet improves, and if the money generates cash flow, the whole credit improves. Some companies that issued equity in 2009 and 2010 include El Paso Pipeline Partners, L.P., and Host Hotels & Resorts, L.P., which is a real estate investment trust (REIT) that owns the real estate of different hotel properties including Marriott. Surprisingly, many of the automotive suppliers, including Tenneco, Dana, TRW, and American Axle, were able to issue equity. The issuances were positive credit events and surprisingly positive equity events. Figure 19.3 shows what happened to Host Hotels' bonds after the April 2009 equity offer.

Figure 19.3   Host Hotels & Resorts 6.75% Due 2016 Bond Price

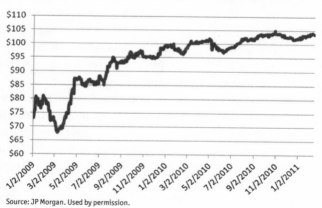

Source: JP Morgan. Used by permission.

Called Debt and Tendered Debt

Calls and tender offers are not insignificant in the junk bond market. When a corporate bond is issued, it often has provisions in its indenture to allow it to buy back the bonds at a set premium price at a specific time in the future. This is known as a *call provision*. The premium declines as the bonds get closer to maturity. There are often reasons the company would like to purchase the bonds at a premium to where they are trading and not rely on the call provision. The action to buy those bonds is known as a *tender*, which the bondholder can either accept or reject. There were 329 tender offers of all issues in the first 11 months of 2010, totaling nearly $50 billion.[2] In addition, there were another $45 billion of bonds called between January and November 2010.

MERGERS AND ACQUISITIONS

Though the above five occurrences can result in capital gains, the acquisition of a junk bond company by a higher-rated operating company is often the best-case scenario for a huge capital gain. Oftentimes, industry competitors, suppliers, or customers want to acquire a junk bond issuing company to enhance business prospects either by reducing competition or improving some aspect of sales or the cost structure. After the acquisition, the junk bond company debt becomes the debt obligation of the higher-rated acquirer. The new company could issue debt at a far lower cost of capital than the coupon on the acquired junk debt. The new company usually calls the old debt, if currently callable, or tenders (makes a generous offer to existing bondholders at the option of each bondholder) for the old junk debt. Two such examples include US Oncology and Psychiatric Solutions.

US Oncology (see Figure 19.4), a B-rated leading cancer care service provider, was bought by McKesson in December 2010, the A-rated healthcare giant. With fiscal year 2009 sales of nearly $109 billion, McKesson is the fourteenth largest overall company in the United States[3] and the largest healthcare company in the world.[4] US Oncology matches its clients with a robust network of oncologists and services. US Oncology's revenue has grown from $2.5 billion in sales in 2005 to $3.5 billion in 2009. Its earnings have remained steady over this time.

The 9.125% due 2017 bonds were trading at $108 before the announcement, and McKesson is tendering for them at $123. While US Oncology had a $101 put, it made far more sense to tender the bonds at $123.

Psychiatric Solutions (see Figure 19.5) is a leading provider of psychiatric healthcare services in the United States. It operates 94 psychiatric hospitals in 32 states, Puerto Rico, and the U.S. Virgin Islands.

Figure 19.4 US Oncology 9.125% Due 2017 Bond Price

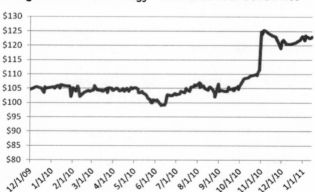

Source: JP Morgan. Used by permission.

Figure 19.5 Psychiatric Solutions 7.75% Due 2015 Bond Price

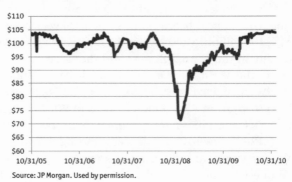

Source: JP Morgan. Used by permission.

In 2009, it had $1.8 billion in revenue, up from $689 million in 2005. Likewise, its earnings have advanced at that same rate. Psychiatric Solutions had B-rated 7.75% due 2015 bonds that were trading in the mid-1990s. The company was acquired by BB-rated Universal Health who promptly called the bonds at its call price of $104.

· WHAT WE KNOW ·

A major benefit of investing in good Strong-Horse companies is that often good things happen to them that drive up the bond price dramatically. Good companies with the proper size and earnings growth:

1. Get upgraded.

2. Become rising stars, resulting in a huge capital gain.

3. Get taken over by a higher-rated, often an investment grade, company, that tenders for the bonds at a significant premium.

4. Issue stock.

CHAPTER 20

THE UGLY AND THE BAD: CCC INVESTING

The musician Pete Seeger put to music words adapted from the book of Ecclesiastes (the song was popularized by the group The Byrds in 1965):

> To everything (turn, turn, turn)
> There is a season (turn, turn, turn)
> And a time to every purpose under the heaven
> A time to be born, a time to die
> A time to buy CCC bonds, and a time to weep

Actually, the last line is mine, but it introduces the topic of investing in CCC bonds.

Most bad and ugly companies fall into the CCC category, which will be our focus. (Although some of the companies that we discuss may be in the B category, most of them are CCC companies.)

There is a fine line between ugly and bad bonds, and many unfortunate events could cause ugly and bad bonds to fail. When a company defaults, there is a wide range of recovery values you could receive for the bond you are holding; you could get 50 cents on the dollar or you could get nothing. According to J.P. Morgan, there were 41 companies that defaulted in 2010, impacting $19 billion of debt (this is in contrast to the terrible 2009 year in which 120 companies defaulted affecting $185 billion of debt). Some of the larger defaults in 2010 included the movie rental companies Blockbuster ($930 million) and Movie Gallery ($540 million) and the tabloid publisher American Media, Inc. (AMI), whose publications include the *National Enquirer* and *Star*.

As I said before, an ugly company could have either a good business model and a bad balance sheet or a good balance sheet and a risky business model. An ugly company could get downgraded, which would raise its cost of capital and potentially lower its bond price. There were 258 downgrades affecting $216 billion of debt in 2010. A company that has been downgraded from investment grade to junk status is called a *fallen angel*. There was $28 billion of debt downgraded to junk status in 2010. Some notable downgrades in 2010 included AIG, the insurance company bailed out by U.S. taxpayers; Sprint Nextel; and several utilities such as Energy Futures Holdings, Edison International, and Dynegy.

Of course, ugly companies may succeed too. The basic business can be salvaged, and we can find a scenario for recovery. There is too much debt relative to the value of the company, but with business improvements and financial engineering, an ugly company has a chance of recovery.

Bad companies, however, typically have a failed business model. Debt is far greater than the value of the business, and even buying the bonds at a steep discount contains too much risk. Movie Gallery is a good example. At its peak, Movie Gallery had 4,700 outlets in North America under the names Movie Gallery, Hollywood Video, and Game Crazy. It was slow, however, to adapt to Netflix and movies on demand. It entered bankruptcy in 2007, but it emerged with too much debt. It tried Chapter 11 of the bankruptcy code again, and it finally liquidated under Chapter 7. Bondholders received next to nothing back.

INVESTING IN CCC BONDS

An investor must be shrewd to successfully invest in CCC bonds: there is a time to be invested in them, and there is a time to be divested of them. As you now know, CCC bonds are the riskiest bonds before bankruptcy. These companies are usually (but not always) high financial risk and low business risk deals. Not all CCC bonds are the same. Some cannot be saved, and you should not invest in them (the bad). For example, I would not invest in the buyout of Billy's Messengering service by Millie in Chapter 5. You should wait and see the projected synergies come to fruition. Otherwise, she may not generate enough cash for debt service.

Volatility is greater for the riskiest bonds, so that during turbulent times these bonds drop in price more than their higher quality brethren. During periods of high default, CCC bonds have performed poorly (exactly as we would expect). If one were to measure returns and volatility for the market for a period ending at or near the peak of default activity—in this case, the end of 2008 when the markets crashed—it is reasonable to expect that returns look worse for CCCs. Let's compare the 10-year returns for the different indices of the high yield market at the end of 2008 (near the market bottom when junk bond prices plummeted) shown in Table 20.1 and at the end of 2010, after two strong years, shown in Table 20.2. Notice how the CCC bond index went from being the worst-performing index to far and away the best: investing in CCC bonds is all about timing.

Table 20.1

Ten-Year Return for High Yield Indices, Ending December 31, 2008

	RETURN
HY Market	23.5%
BB	42.7%
B	17.2%
CCC	−4.7%
S&P 500	−13.0%

Note: The high yield market and other high yield indices are defined by the Bank of America Merrill Lynch U.S. Constrained Indices with the Master, BB, B, and CCC with index identifications of HUC0, HUC1, HUC2, and HUC3, respectively.

Source: BoA Merrill Lynch High Yield Bond Indices. Used by permission.

Table 20.2

Ten-Year Return for High Yield Indices, Ending December 31, 2010

	RETURN
HY Market	131.3%
BB	129.4%
B	109.7%
CCC	196.7%
S&P 500	15.0%

Note: The high yield market and other high yield indices are defined by the Bank of America Merrill Lynch U.S. Constrained Indices with the Master, BB, B, and CCC with index identifications of HUC0, HUC1, HUC2, and HUC3, respectively.

Source: BoA Merrill Lynch High Yield Bond Indices. Used by permission.

Remember, in the case of a bankruptcy, bondholders are paid *before* stockholders, regardless of the bond's rating. You would expect bonds to be less volatile and offer a lower return than stocks due to their increased security. However, that is not the case. CCC bonds have greater volatility and higher returns than the S&P 500 Index because all the securities are of risky credits, while the S&P 500 is made up of far less risky credits on average (see Table 20.3).

Table 20.3 Volatilities of CCC Index and Equities

	5 YEAR	10 YEAR
CCC	22.0%	18.1%
S&P 500	17.6%	16.3%

Note: Data are as of the end of November 2010.

Source: *JPMorgan 2010 High Yield Annual Review.*

Different time periods also tell different stories. CCC bonds perform better at the end of a recovery period and worse when the economy is in a recession or slump. In a scenario of an improving economy and better market liquidity where credit spreads revert to historic averages, I would expect CCCs to perform well despite defaults. In fact, there is typically a pattern of relative performance. During periods of economic distress, such as 2008, CCCs are the first to decline, and they decline the most, relative to B and BB bonds. During a recovery, first BB bonds recover, and CCC bonds lag behind. When the difference in yield is overwhelming, CCC bonds recover and with a vengeance. In 2009, for example, CCC bonds returned more than 112% compared to 58% for the high yield market as Table 20.4 shows.

Table 20.4 Annual Returns for High Yield Indices

	2008	2009	2010
HY Market	−26.1%	58.1%	15.1%
BB	−18.9%	44.9%	14.3%
B	−28.1%	48.9%	13.8%
CCC	−41.7%	112.8%	19.9%

Note: The high yield market and other high yield indexes are defined by the Bank of America Merrill Lynch U.S. Constrained Indices with the Master, BB, B, and CCC with index identifications of HUC0, HUC1, HUC2, and HUC3, respectively.

Source: BoA Merrill Lynch High Yield Bond Indices. Used by permission.

The Lehman Brothers bankruptcy in September 2008 scared the markets in a manner not seen in the lifetime of professional money managers or brokers. Hedge funds seized up, not allowing investors to pull their money out. A money market fund broke the sacrosanct $1 per share level. Investors felt they had a limited ability to access a safe haven in anything but Treasury bonds or overnight CDs of the highest-quality banks, such as J.P. Morgan. High-quality issuers could not raise money; banks and security firms were being bailed out by the federal government. Security prices all fell, especially the riskiest credits (that is, CCC credits).

While patterns are important, selecting the correct credit in which to invest is more important. When dealing with individual securities, you are not buying the market, you are lending to a company. *The best time to invest in junk bonds is when the market is hurting and bonds can be bought at very low prices.* Only invest, though, if you apply the Strong-Horse Method: look at sizes, trends, earnings, leverages, and coverages (and, if possible, covenants). Sometimes you can achieve a great return. The following are four examples of ugly bonds in which the businesses were fundamentally strong, debt leverage was high, and the investment results vastly different. I will give you examples of two winners and two losers.

Two Successes

Univision Communications is the leading Spanish-language media company in the United States.[1] A consortium—Broadcasting Media Partners, Inc., of Madison Dearborn Partners; Providence Equity Partners; the Texas Pacific Group; Thomas H. Lee Partners; and the Saban Capital Group—acquired Univision in 2007. With revenue of nearly $2 billion in 2009, Univision has had relatively stable sales and earnings since 2007.

During the fourth quarter of 2008, with the credit markets in disarray, Univision's high leverage (13.5 times in 2008), its low coverage (barely 1.0 times), and the prevailing terrible advertising market for broadcasting forced the 9.75% issue down. Additionally, it was in the midst of a major four-year lawsuit with Mexican media giant Grupo Televisa, threatening the loss of Televisa's coveted soap operas. Under the new private equity sponsors, Univision reported a huge $5.1 billion loss because of a $5.4 billion noncash write-off for impairment of goodwill.

However, the 9.75% due 2015 was able to fully recover from its lows in the teens (Figure 20.1). The recovery was due to many factors, including the increased advertising market for Spanish-language broadcasting (coinciding with the high population growth of Spanish-language viewers in the United States) and the stability of its operating earnings in 2009. Univision ended its lawsuit with Televisa and agreed to pay hefty

Figure 20.1 Univision 9.75% Due 2015 Bond Price*

*Bond also listed as Univision 9.75%/10.5% due 2015.

Source: JP Morgan. Used by permission.

royalty fees for use of its content. Additionally, Univision's negotiated retransmission consent fees—charges to the cable provider on a per-user basis—contributed to its earnings growth since that time. These factors combined to lead Univision to a recovery throughout 2009 and beyond.

Note, at the time of this writing, the company is still risky with leverage of 12.3 times for the previous 12 months and coverage of 1.5 times for the first 9 months of 2010—poor for a corporate credit trading at par and still a cause of concern today.

Freescale Semiconductor, a leading semiconductor manufacturer in the United States, also worked out well. The company was originally formed as a spin off by telecommunications giant Motorola, Inc., in 2004. It was acquired in late 2006 by a syndicate of private equity investors including the Blackstone Group, the Carlyle Group, TPG Capital, and funds advised by Permira Advisers. Freescale's 2010 sales of $4.5 billion rank it as the sixteenth largest semiconductor supplier in the world, according to iSuppli Corporation. Freescale's sales have declined—and earnings have been volatile—since 2006.

Technology companies are notoriously volatile and sensitive to the economy. As the recession worsened, Freescale's EBITDA dropped from $2.2 billion to $811 million in 2009. Its revenues were nearly cut in half over that time. Its product line was particularly hard hit as sales to the Big Three U.S. auto producers plummeted in 2009. That year was tough for auto sales and caused both GM and Chrysler to enter bankruptcy. Freescale avoided bankruptcy through deft financial engineering, purchasing existing debt at a huge discount, which reduced total debt by $2.3 billion (down from $9.5 billion), and hoarded cash. In addition, throughout 2009, it showed sequential improvement, and improved factory utilization (see Figure 20.2).

Figure 20.2 Freescale 10.125% Due 2016 Bond Price

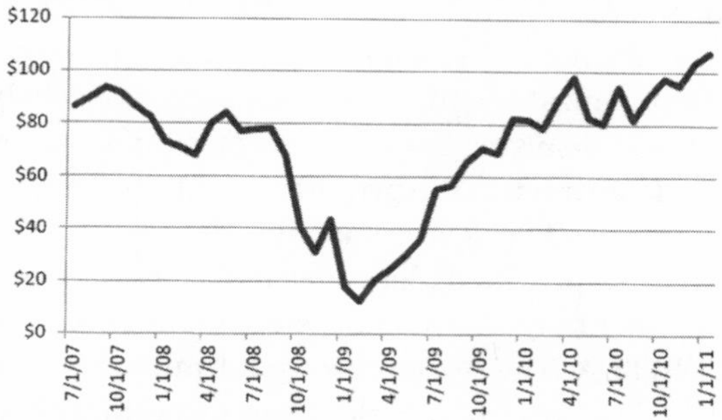

Source: JP Morgan. Used by permission.

As part of the financial restructuring, it offered a new bond to its current investors at a better position in the capital structure. All of the above led to a feeling that Freescale would survive. The issue was trading above par by the end of 2010. It had leverage of only 5.3 times and coverage of 2.4 times. Both are good numbers for a CCC-rated bond.

Two Failures

The case of **LyondellBasell Industries (LBI)**, one of the largest plastics, chemical, and refining companies in the world,[2] is an example of how the location of your investment within the capital structure can determine your recovery in bankruptcy. Basell Polyolefins acquired Lyondell Chemical in 2007 to form LBI. The consolidated debt from its acquisition by Basell reached about $24 billion, up from $8 billion prior to the acquisition. That debt increase was bad enough, but business risk increased as both the economy turned south and raw material prices took an adverse turn. A significant reduction in margins and profits left LBI unable to meet its liquidity needs.[3] High leverage, the decline in the volume of business, and poor margins led LBI's U.S. operations to file for Chapter 11 bankruptcy in January 2009.

The reorganization process during bankruptcy helped LBI tremendously, cleansing the company of significant legacy liabilities and contracts. In April 2010, LBI officially emerged from bankruptcy. The development of the shale gas industry in North America provided a cheaper feedstock supply for LBI. This fundamentally improved the company's margins, profits, and EBITDA. The stock price went from $15 to nearly $35 in 2010 and secured bondholders received more than their full principal back. However, the deeply subordinated 8.375% senior bondholders received an unfortunate combination of cash, equity, and a residual litigation claim (see Figure 20.3). The 8.375% bonds as of this writing are trading at about 45% of original par due to the increased value of the equity and the litigation claim. Lyondell was an ugly investment that failed.

Figure 20.3 LyondellBasell 8.375% Due 2015 Bond Price*

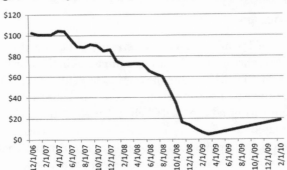

*Bond also known as Nell AF Sarl 8.375% due 2015.

Source: JP Morgan. Used by permission.

Aleris International is a major aluminum manufacturer based in Beachwood, Ohio, with over 40 production facilities worldwide.[4] Aleris is another cyclical company sensitive to commodity prices with too much debt that could not withstand an economic downturn. Prior to bankruptcy, the company was purchased by the private equity firm TPG Capital, which placed substantial debt on its books. Aleris experienced growth in sales from 2005 to 2008 when it ran into trouble by anticipating that aluminum prices would continue to rise over the long term. It was hit by the global recession, led by decreased demand from its customers: North American building and construction companies, American and European automotive companies, and distribution and transportation companies. Due to the nature of the aluminum production industry, Aleris held significant inventory. Aluminum prices—as well as oil, steel, and other commodities—plummeted in late 2008 and early 2009. With nearly $2.7 billion of long-term debt on its books, Aleris filed for bankruptcy in February 2009 after it was no longer able to cover its interest expense.

In February 2010, private equity and hedge fund companies Oaktree, Apollo, and Sankaty announced their $690 million acquisition of Aleris from TPG.[5] They were successful in getting the court to eliminate most of its debt including the 9% and 10% bonds. With the recovery, the company's new private equity buyers issued new debt with the majority of the proceeds going to pay themselves a dividend. Aleris has recovered impressively since reemergence due to improved demand, decreased interest expense from the reorganization, and a cost savings initiative called the Aleris Operating System (AOS)—an initiative of principles and operating practices to improve efficiency and reduce costs. The AOS generated $140 million of permanent cost savings in the 12 months ending September 30,

Figure 20.4 Aleris 10% Due 2016 Bond Price

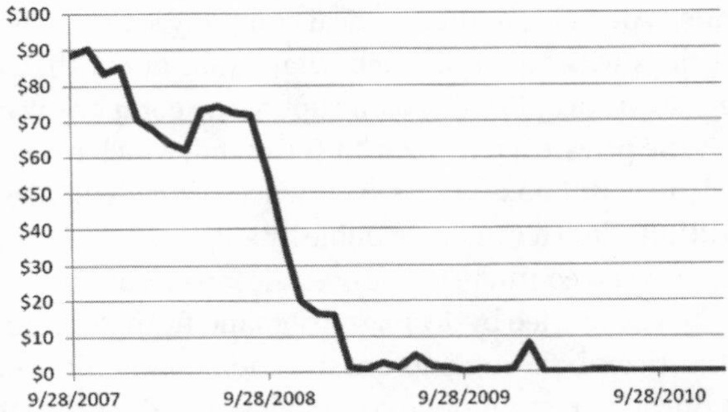

Source: JP Morgan. Used by permission.

2010. Additionally, Aleris had leverage of 2.5 times and coverage of 4.0 times for that same period. However, the 10% bonds of 2016 are now worthless (see Figure 20.4). From the perspective of the bondholder, this investment was a bad one.

CCCs and LBOs (Buyer Beware)

There are times, as I have said, when CCC investing can show impressive returns. Most CCC leveraged buyouts are of companies that have acceptable business risk but high financial risk and high covenant risk. Like high yield investing in general, buying bonds of LBOs results in better returns when spreads are wide (low price), capital is scarce, and defaults are high. Such was the case in 2008 and 2009. During those times, and using the Strong-Horse Method, one can create positions at significantly more attractive valuations than at times when the opposite conditions—narrow spreads, plentiful capital, and low defaults—prevail.

Private equity participants continue to exploit the market inefficiencies. They issue debt when rates are low, covenants are loose, and demand is high. Underwriters benefit during these times because they generate their revenues through volume. As market insiders, underwriters are supposed to conduct due diligence and make sure there is adequate disclosure of the risks to the investors. While there may be some disclosure, often its importance is not highlighted.

THE BAD: COMPANIES THAT FAIL

In the worst cases these companies have failing businesses (similar to the yellow pages businesses in Chapter 6) in which the value of the company is far less than the debt supporting it. Their leverage is high, and typically the expected value that debt holders will receive is negligible in the event of a default. These companies are different from the Lyondell example because that company was able to emerge from bankruptcy and bondholders lost most but not all of their investment.

The Strong-Horse Method will keep you away from investing in these companies. The bonds are probably cheap, but they should get cheaper as the prices decline. Generally, only investors in bankrupt and distressed securities should look at these companies.

• WHAT WE KNOW •

1. There is a time to buy CCC bonds when above average returns can be achieved, typically after a major market selloff when prices have fallen too far.

2. Strong-Horse Investing can calibrate the risk you are taking in investing in ugly bonds.

3. Bad bonds should be avoided for all but distressed debt investors.

CHAPTER 21

INVESTING IN AND ANALYZING A JUNK BOND MUTUAL FUND

Junk bond investing is difficult to do for the individual investor because it is mostly an institutional market. Putting a portfolio together of good companies requires dealing with multiple brokers. It used to require buying in blocks of $250,000 at a minimum, but now, with the proliferation of discount and online brokers, that is no longer a requirement. One can buy junk bonds in much smaller sizes as long as your broker clears you as being suitable. A recent perusal of a major discount broker's website showed more than 1,000 names available for transaction. Generally, broker spreads are higher (that is, you pay a higher price) for the small investor. For these reasons, among others, a professional manager is an acceptable alternative to a self-directed portfolio. Finding the correct manager, however, requires careful consideration.

The growth of the junk bond market since the 1970s fueled the development of a healthy and robust junk bond mutual fund industry, starting with a few funds in the early 1980s and burgeoning to 300 funds currently. Just as the early days of the junk bond market resembled the Wild West, so too did the early days of junk bond mutual funds. In fact, one junk bond fund manager went to jail, and several others were barred from the industry for life (primarily for taking warrants in their personal accounts from Drexel Burnham in takeover deals financed by Drexel). The phenomenal growth of junk bond mutual funds has taken junk bonds from a small insular group of institutional investors into the living rooms and 401(k) investments of retail and retirees across the United States.

While mutual funds may provide an untrained investor with the comfort of professional management and diversification, these pooled portfolios have proliferated in number and style, attracting some managers without the requisite skill and expertise. As a result, navigating the waters of junk bond mutual funds without a basic understanding of fund management can often be treacherous. I can relate to the experience of the novice investor in junk bond mutual funds based on my own experience in sailing.

Sailing is great if you know what you are doing but dangerous if you don't. Most times you do not get from point A to point B by sailing in a straight line. How you get there depends on the wind. Oftentimes you have to *tack*, that is, move in several directions to get to your final destination. Sometimes you have to alter your course because of constantly changing circumstances. I learned to sail in New York Harbor on the Hudson River. In one lesson, I was intent on reaching the Statue of

Liberty, not realizing it was a federally protected site. I aimed my boat toward Lady Liberty. The sailing instructor kept getting more nervous, yelling, "Bob, tack," "Bob, turn the boat," and finally my son (remember him?) grabbed the controls and shifted course.

I was tacking nicely, but my objectives were all wrong. I did not know that at a federally protected site, trespassers could be shot by U.S. soldiers. I was determined but unaware of that crucial information. Fortunately, my sailing instructor was aware of it.

Just as in sailing, shifting course is important in portfolio management. Midcourse corrections are very common in managing a high yield portfolio. If the economy is improving at a rapid pace, you should tilt your portfolio toward taking more credit risk in your high yield investments. If the economy is entering a slower or negative phase, it is important to reduce credit risk. It is not enough to simply stay with your strategy regardless of the world around you.

A bond matures and is worth par at maturity while a bond fund never matures because it constantly reinvests its cash in new investments. Therefore, investing in a bond fund is *unlike* investing in a bond. While the number of years to maturity is a key component in investment grade bond analytics, it is only secondarily important to credit analysis in junk bond analytics. However, in my opinion, a junk bond fund should exhibit more sensitivity to rising interest rates than an individual junk bond. When interest rates rise, high grade bonds and bond funds drop in price with the longer maturity bonds suffering the most. Individual junk bonds also drop in price but less so for three reasons:

1. More of the return comes from the higher coupon junk bond advantage.

2. Generally, higher rates are correlated with a stronger economy, which enhances the upgrade prospects of junk bond issuers.

3. Individual junk bonds have a relatively shorter maturity.

A Fund's Objectives

Understanding a fund's objectives is critical when purchasing a fund. These objectives are spelled out in detail in the *prospectus*. Just as my objective of reaching the Statue of Liberty was uninformed and potentially dangerous, so too is investing in funds whose objectives are not consistent with your risk tolerance. A prospectus is a document required by the SEC for all public offerings. It includes a lot of information about the fund, including its objectives.

A mutual fund prospectus may say that the fund objective is "to achieve high current yield." This statement means that the fund should invest to provide investors a high monthly income check. Unfortunately, some fund managers interpret that objective to mean, "Invest in those securities that yield the most." On the surface that idea seems innocent enough: find bonds yielding 11% or 12% or even 15% and buy them. That strategy encourages fund managers to seek riskier bonds whose prices are discounted from par. Generally, those bonds are considered stressed and have a higher projected default rate. In the event of a default, the bond price will fall even more and the coupon stream will be eliminated. There are successful strategies for investing in distressed securities, but the fund objective should point out that the strategy is focused on distressed credit investing.

I would prefer a fund objective to be "seek high total return," which the managers will accomplish through a combination of current yield and capital gains. To achieve this objective, the fund managers are willing to invest in higher-quality, lower-yielding "credits." The theory behind this move is that by investing in higher-quality companies, the bond price may rise as creditworthiness improves and that a combination of capital gains and coupons may provide an acceptable total return. The Strong-Horse strategy does just that: it calibrates a company's creditworthiness and looks for a combination of coupon income and capital gains.

You now know that not all junk bond funds are the same and that the performance of these funds may be quite different. If you do not believe me, I will prove it. One difference is simply based on the strategy of each manager.

I personally learned to analyze a fund before investing in it the hard way many years ago when I purchased a diversified small-cap growth stock fund from a major brokerage house. I did not do my homework before investing (after all, aren't all small-cap funds the same? No!). The fund performed poorly. When I finally began to analyze the fund to assess my losses, I realized that it was invested 60% in oil and oil-related industries at a time when oil prices were declining precipitously.

Imagine my outrage at having lost money on this investment! In my mind, that fund was not diversified. When I took this matter up with the fund manager, and, inevitably, its legal counsel, the firm lawyers made the case to me that there are many oil service industries and the fund had met the SEC-mandated diversification rules. The fund was legally diversified, but it was not diversified from an investor's perspective.

PROOF THAT ALL JUNK BOND FUNDS ARE NOT THE SAME

The high yield market melted 26% in 2008 and recovered 58% in 2009. We are going to look at the best and worst managers in 2008 and see how they performed in the recovery year. Then we will combine performance for both years. A list of the 10 best and worst performers for the two years is in the Appendix.

As shown in Table 21.1, the worst junk bond performance in 2008 lost 79% of its assets, while the best lost only 6%. That 73% difference is a staggering number. You might say that perhaps the difference was caused by an unusual outlier. So, look at the average of the 10 best and 10 worst performances that year as shown in Table 21.2. This number is still too large, proving that manager selection played a major role.

There should be adequate disclosure to make an informed investment. Let's look at the disclosure of three of the worst per-

Table 21.1 Best and Worst Junk Bond Performances for 2008

	2008 RETURNS
Best Performer	−5.8%
Worst Performer	−78.7%
Difference	−72.9%

Source: Lipper, a Thompson Reuters company. Used with permission.

Table 21.2 Average of the 10 Best and
10 Worst Junk Bond Performances for 2008

AVERAGE	2008 RETURNS
10 Best	–11.4%
10 Worst	–44.3%
Difference	–32.9%
Source: Lipper, a Thompson Reuters company. Used with permission.	

forming junk bond funds reported by Lipper for the one-year period in 2008 and contrast them. We will look at the Oppenheimer Champion Fund, the Highland High Income Fund, and the John Hancock High Yield Fund. The disclosure of the Highland Fund was adequate. However, shareholders filed suit against the Oppenheimer Fund specifically alleging poor disclosure. It would be your fault if you invested in a fund that performed poorly but adequately disclosed a strategy unsuitable to your investment objectives. *You should not invest in a fund with poor disclosure.*

Figure 21.1 charts the 10 best and 10 worst high yield mutual fund performers in 2008 and their performance the following recovery year. The figure also combines the two-year performance. It shows that the best 2008 performers also had the best cumulative two-year performance.

Notice that even with excellent 2009 returns, the worst 2008 performers still had weak or negative returns at the end of the two-year period. Losses hurt more than gains help—if you lose 50% one year, you have to be up 100% the next year to be back at even. *Note:* Fund S had no 2009 performance because the fund folded at the beginning of 2009.

Figure 21.1 2008's 10 Best and 10 Worst Mutual Funds over a Two-Year Performance

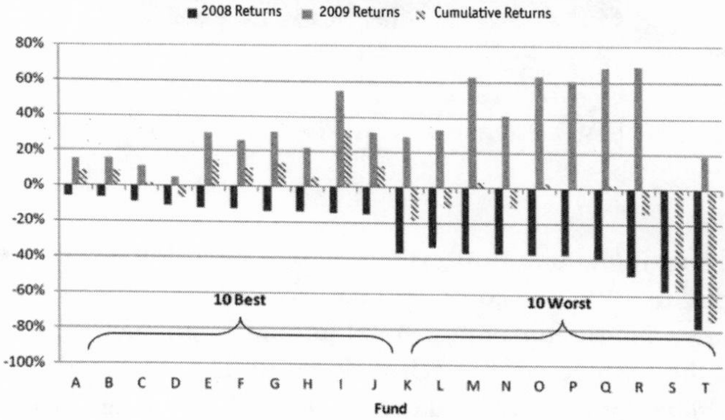

Source: Lipper, a Thompson Reuters company. Used with permission.

Oppenheimer Champion Fund

The more fund disclosure, the better. The information has to be complete, informative, and accurate. The worst performing junk bond fund in 2008 reported by Lipper was the Oppenheimer Champion Fund, down nearly 80%! In a lawsuit filed against Oppenheimer Management—the management company running the Champion Fund—the plaintiff investors alleged that the company did not adequately disclose that the fund invested heavily in illiquid derivative instruments.[1] A *derivative* is a financial instrument (or, more simply, a contractual agreement between two parties) that has a value, based on the expected future price movements of the asset to which it is linked—called the *underlying asset*—such as a stock share or a currency.

Not all fund fact sheets include the size of the fund or the percent of the fund invested in the lowest bond category. This information, however, is crucial to investing in the high yield asset class.

Highland High Income Fund

In contrast to the Oppenheimer Champion Fund's lacking information, the disclosure of the second worst performer in 2008, the Highland High Income Fund, supplied adequate information for an investor to make an informed decision. It included the following information:

Size of fund: $5 million

Number of holdings: 8

Average quality of securities: Caa1 to Caa2

Distribution of ratings: 70% in the Caa sector

Objective: High current income while seeking to preserve shareholder capital

Illiquid investment: Up to 15%

A $5 million fund is too small. The goal of a professionally managed, diversified high yield fund is to be large enough so that if any one investment defaults, it will not materially impact fund performance. A $5 million fund with only 8 holdings is too small. I would prefer a fund with at least 100 holdings. Remember, a defaulted bond could lose more than 50% of value from par. Also, a $5 million fund is too small to absorb all of the expenses (many of which are fixed and independent of fund size).

The Highland Fund was heavily invested in the Caa credit quality, which was a bullish strategy based on an improving economic environment. Unfortunately, the economy nosedived into almost the second Great Depression. This sector was heavily hit, and as a result, the fund was one of the worst performers that year. Unfortunately, Highland closed the fund and was not able to experience the run up in securities prices in 2009. The Caa sector rose that year more than 100%.

Despite abysmal performance, the disclosure was adequate. Management did what it said it would do: "invest for high current income." With that information, an informed investor could make a determination as to invest or not.

John Hancock High Yield Fund

The third worst performer in 2008 was the John Hancock High Yield Fund. Disclosure was adequate, and there appears to be an explanation for the 2008, 2009, and subsequent performance. Both the prospectus and annual report state the fund's investment objective as this: "Seek high current income. Capital appreciation is a secondary goal." Thus, the fund is stating clearly that the primary goal is income. As I stated before, this means buying lower rated, higher yielding investments. Prior to the 2008 meltdown, the fund had 42% in the riskiest CCC and not rated bonds. This sector was devastated the most. In 2009, with the market recovering, the manager had 55% of the portfolio in that sector, showing the greatest improvement, which is the reason why Hancock was one of the best performing funds in 2009. It appears that the strategy of emphasizing the lowest rated (lowest priced, highest yielding) bonds hurt them in 2008 and helped them in 2009.

PERFORMANCE COMPARISONS

Some managers are substantially better than others in certain markets. As an investor, you must look at the track record of the fund and understand the investment style of the manager. These stark differences in performance prove that the selection of an appropriate junk bond fund manager is important. Care must be taken to select the right manager, so you need adequate disclosure and an understanding of the manager based on that disclosure.

The 2008 worst performers were the most aggressive that year. They declined so much that despite a great 2009 recovery, they were still down 15% for the two-year period. The best performers in 2008 were the worst performers in 2009 because they had the highest quality portfolios and were not able to take advantage of the spectacular recovery in bonds rated CCC that year. However, the best performers had a positive performance for the two-year period. The Strong-Horse Method slightly underperformed the 2008 BoA Merrill Lynch High Yield Index, but it more than fully recovered in the two-year period.

To see the difference over the two years, the best way to display and compare the results is to start with a hypothetical

Table 21.3 Cumulative Performance Comparison
for 2007 Through 2009

	12/31/07	12/31/08	12/31/09
2008 10 Best	$100.00	$88.32	$109.35
2008 10 Worst	$100.00	$56.27	$85.06
S&P 500	$100.00	$63.00	$79.67
BoA Merrill Lynch	$100.00	$73.89	$116.82
Strong Horse	$100.00	$70.53	$115.96

Sources: Lipper, a Thompson Reuters company; BoA Merrill Lynch High Yield Bond Indices; and Nomura Corporate Research and Asset Management, High Yield Total Return Institutional Composite (HYTRIC). Used by permission.

$100 on December 31, 2007, and see how much you would have at close on December 31, 2009.

EXCHANGE-TRADED FUNDS

An exchange-traded fund (ETF) is a collection of securities bundled together to mimic an index. A high yield bond ETF would mimic a high yield bond index. An example of two ETFs and their mimicked indices is shown in Table 21.4.

Table 21.4 Two ETFs and Their Mimicked Indices

TICKER	INDEX
JNK	Barclays Capital High Yield Very Liquid Index
HYG	iBoxx $ Liquid High Yield Index

An investor would buy or sell the ETF just as any stock. The fund is not managed, but it is designed to provide a high yield market return. Because the asset class is so volatile, I personally have trouble with any junk bond fund that is not managed. However, if you are positive on the market, an ETF is an acceptable approach.

Shorting Exchange-Traded Funds

Remember, an investor would buy or sell an ETF just as any other stock. Many institutional investors hedge their market risk by using credit analysis research skills to invest in specific credits and "shorting the ETF." When you *short a security,* you hope the security's price drops. To short, the investor borrows the security from a broker, pays a fee for the borrow, and then sells that security at the current price. At a later time, the investor purchases the security (in this case the ETF) to "cover" the short and unwind the trade.

An example here may help. Normally, you purchase a security and hope it goes up. The reverse is true for a short. You want to borrow the security when the price is high and cover by buying it back at a low price. For example, say the market today is $50, and you think it is going down. You borrow and sell the security at $50. Days later, it is trading at $40. You purchase the security at $40 and use the purchase to repay the borrow, thus making a $10 profit. (There are, however, many costs along the way that I will not discuss here.)

STEPS TO BUYING A MUTUAL FUND

Throughout this chapter I have provided suggestions on how to invest and analyze a junk bond mutual fund. When actually buying the fund, make sure to follow these steps:

1. Read the prospectus.

2. Ask to see the fund fact sheet.

3. For any missing information, such as a credit quality breakdown, check websites such as Morningstar.

· WHAT WE KNOW ·

1. Investing in a junk bond fund has similarities and differences to investing in junk bonds. In both cases, credit is the key factor for success. What is different is that a fund has no final maturity while a bond does.

2. All junk bond funds are different.

3. Read the prospectus objectives.

4. If your goal is to take credit risk, to take advantage of a growing economy for example, the fund would invest in the highest yielding, riskiest credits. The prospectus objective would say, "Seek high current yield."

5. If your goal is a longer-term balanced asset class investment in junk bonds in all economic times, the fund should invest in a broad cross-section of bonds. The fund prospectus would say, "Seek total return through a combination of current yield and capital appreciation."

6. Do not try to sail directly to federally protected landmarks.

A STRONG HORSE WILL PULL YOU THROUGH

The junk bond market is an established part of the capital markets. While extreme risk takers will always exist, the market is no longer dominated by such investors. Investing in this asset class involves use of credit analysis to take advantage of the extra yield these securities offer, and the best way to do so is to utilize the Strong-Horse Method discussed throughout this book.

Lending to BB, B, and CCC credits, if done successfully, can be profitable—that is the junk bond advantage. Lending $1,000 at a 10% interest rate (equivalent to a CCC credit) and getting your money back at maturity is equivalent to a 10% return. That $1,000 doubles in a little more than 7 years, and it is worth nearly $2,600 in 10 years. All you need to do is lend to companies that do not default. If you lent that same amount at a 5% interest rate (equivalent to a BBB credit), it would be worth only $1,407 after 7 years and $1,630 after 10 years. Treasury bonds or AAA bonds, while safer, offer a lower return. Compounding over time is powerful, and it is what provides the strength of junk bond investing.

The easiest way to lose money in junk bonds is to buy the bonds of a company that then defaults. The Strong-Horse Method helps you avoid such a situation. Look for companies whose creditworthiness is improving, and avoid declining credits. This book gives some benchmarks for investing, but remember, they are only benchmarks. Fund managers specializing in this asset class have to be fully invested; you do not. There is a time to take risk, and there is a time to take your money off the table and wait for better markets. In general, when high yield spreads are 250 basis points or less, stay out of the market; it is too rich. You can only lose at those spreads. When the market is 600 basis points or more, most likely you will be successful.

Improving credits are those that have increasing profits and cash flow and lower debt levels. If the company has market share leadership and cost controls and it generates excess cash flow, there is a lower chance of default than if it had negative trends. History has shown that these good companies offer the possibility of recovery greater than par before the maturity date. *Good things happen to good companies.* These companies can be acquired by a higher-rated company who tenders for the bonds at a premium. The companies also have access to the equity market. Equity offerings fundamentally improve a company's balance sheet and bond price.

Some investments, especially CCC investments, are quite risky. As you know, I call them "ugly investments." However, they can provide substantial capital gains if purchased at a discount as well as a high coupon. These investments require considerably more analysis, but the rewards are there along with the risk. For most investors, a negative trend is tantamount to a full stop. A positive business trend in a CCC company is inter-esting; its high interest payments over several years can gener-ate great returns.

Bad investments should be avoided. These companies typ-ically have negative business trends and high debt leverage. Oftentimes, they have obsolete products and not enough capi-tal or time to fix their problems—only specialists should invest in these types of investments.

Millie, while a friend and a great person, does not have enough of a track record with her messengering company after its having been combined with Billy's. Under a negative sce-nario, she would have a negative earnings trend and debt lever-age that was too high. I would not lend to her.

One real problem you now have is what to do with all the money you have earned. After food, shelter, taking care of your family and your retirement, you have options. My suggestion is to take advantage of the power of compounding a high coupon rate and reinvest at least a portion of your money in junk bonds.

APPENDIX

STRONG-HORSE METHOD TRACK RECORD
(FROM CHAPTER 4, "THE JUNK BOND MARKET")

The Nomura Corporate Research and Asset Management (NCRAM) High Yield Total Return Institutional Composite (Table A.1) contains accounts that are aggressively managed for a high level of current income and capital appreciation. The composite was created on September 1, 2008, but the composite's inception dates to 1991.

Table A.1 Total Composite Assets End of Period (in Millions of Dollars)

PERIOD	ASSETS
Q4 1991	$10.2
1992	$37.1
1993	$103.7
1994	$15.4
1995	$111.8
1996	$141.4
1997	$180.1
1998	$257.7
1999	$294.7
2000	$320.0
2001	$419.8
2002	$647.5
2003	$1,345.2
2004	$1,880.4
2005	$2,018.8
2006	$3,059.0
2007	$3,473.8
2008	$2,396.7
2009	$2,747.0
Q1 2010	$2,769.8

STANDARD DEVIATION
(FROM CHAPTER 12, "BOND PRICE VOLATILITY")

Variance and *standard deviation* are statistical measures that quantify the dispersion of returns around the average return. Standard deviation is the square root of variance. We are using a standard deviation based on a sample, not a population (the difference is that the final step is divided by $n-1$ instead of just n). The formula is as follows:

Strategy 1

First take the set of data points:
$\{1, 1, 1, 1, 1, 1, 1, 1, 1, 1, 1, 1\}$
Then, find the mean of those points:
$= 1$

Next, calculate the square of the difference of each point from the data set's mean (1 in this case):

$(1-1)^2 = 0$	$(1-1)^2 = 0$
$(1-1)^2 = 0$	$(1-1)^2 = 0$
$(1-1)^2 = 0$	$(1-1)^2 = 0$
$(1-1)^2 = 0$	$(1-1)^2 = 0$
$(1-1)^2 = 0$	$(1-1)^2 = 0$
$(1-1)^2 = 0$	$(1-1)^2 = 0$

Finally, find the square root of the sum of those values, divided by $n-1$:

$= 0$

Strategy 2

First take the set of data points:
$\{0, 4, -3, 6, -4, 8, -7, 5.5, -2.5, 6, -4, 3\}$
Then, find the mean of those points:
$= 1$

Next, calculate the square of the difference of each point from the data set's mean (1 in this case):

$(0-1)^2 = 1$	$(-7-1)^2 = 64$
$(4-1)^2 = 9$	$(5.5-1)^2 = 20.25$
$(-3-1)^2 = 16$	$(-2.5-1)^2 = 12.25$
$(6-1)^2 = 25$	$(6-1)^2 = 25$
$(-4-1)^2 = 25$	$(-4-1)^2 = 25$
$(8-1)^2 = 49$	$(3-1)^2 = 4$

Finally, find the square root of the sum of those values, divided by $n-1$:

$= 5$

To calculate standard deviation in Microsoft Excel, use the function by entering =STDEV(x:x) into a blank cell, with x:x being the range of your data set.

EBITDA CALCULATIONS
(FROM CHAPTER 9, "AN EXAMPLE OF HOW TO CONDUCT A STRONG-HORSE ANALYSIS")

EBITDA is designed to show a company's earnings before interest, taxes, depreciation, and amortization, but companies like to include noncash items and nonrecurring items (such the gain on a sale of a factory) to boost their EBITDA figures in the eyes of investors. *Adjusted EBITDA* includes these one-time, nonrecurring items. If possible, the goal is to use these numbers in the context of estimating the future. There are two methodologies to calculate EBITDA: starting with revenue and working down (on an income statement) or starting with net income and working up. Let's look at these 12-month 2009 EBITDA calculations for both Owens-Illinois and Solo Cup:

Owens-Illinois

Revenue	$7,067	Net income (loss)	$162
Cost of goods sold	– $5,583	Depreciation and amortization	+ $406
Gross profit	**$1,484**	Interest expense	+ $222
SG&A	– $565	Tax (benefit) provision	+ $128
EBITDA	**$919**	**EBITDA**	**$918**
		Other expense	+ $477
		Other revenue	+ $105
		Adjusted EBITDA	**$1290**

Solo Cup

Revenue	$1,503	Net income (loss)	($36)
Cost of goods sold	– $1,296	Depreciation and amortization	+ $70
Gross profit	**$207**	Interest expense	+ $63
SG&A	– $150	Tax (benefit) provision	+ ($6)
EBITDA	**$57**	**EBITDA**	**$91**
		Impairment of goodwill	+ $17
		Loss on asset disposal	+ $9
		Loss on debt extinguishment	+ $3
		Reclassification of loss	+ $9
		Adjusted EBITDA	**$129**

Why are the two EBITDA methodologies nearly identical for O-I while Solo has a difference of $34 million? Because often-times, but not always, companies in trouble have numerous noncash transactions that impact net income but should not be in a continuing operations EBITDA calculation.

MUTUAL FUND PERFORMANCE
(FROM CHAPTER 21, "INVESTING IN AND ANALYZING A JUNK BOND MUTUAL FUND")

First, Table A.2 gives us a look at the 10 best high yield funds of 2008, the worst performing year for the S&P 500 Index since 1931—the Great Depression. The average performance in 2008 was negative 11.4%.

Table A.2 The 10 Best Performing High Yield Funds for 2008

	2008 RETURN	2009 RETURN
A. Wells Fargo: ST HY B; Inv	−5.8%	15.3%
B. Access One: FX HY; Inv	−6.3%	15.8%
C. Rydex: HY Str; Class A	−8.7%	11.1%
D. Direxion: Dyn HY Bd; Inv	−10.7%	4.8%
E. Direxion: Spect Sel A; Svc	−12.2%	30.0%
F. Intrepid: Income	−12.6%	26.0%
G. Harbor: HY Bond; Inst	−13.7%	30.9%
H. EquiTrust: Str Yld; Class A	−13.8%	22.0%
I. MainStay 130/30 HY; Class I	−14.7%	54.8%
J. MEMBERS: High Income; Class Y	−14.9%	31.5%
Average	**−11.4%**	**24.2%**

Source: Lipper, a Thompson Reuters company. Used by permission.

As shown in Table A.3, the average performance for the 10 worst performing funds in 2008 was negative 44.3%. *The difference between the average best and worst is 33%!* The market recovered the following year. So how did our best and worst performers do in the recovery year and for the two years?

Table A.3 The 10 Worst Performing High Yield Funds for 2008

	2008 RETURN	2009 RETURN
K. Fidelity Real Est High Income	−36.7%	28.8%
L. PowerShares HY Corp Bd	−33.4%	33.0%
M. Pioneer Global HY; Class B	−36.7%	62.8%
N. Sun America: HYB; Class C	−36.9%	41.2%
O. Eaton Vance High Inc; Class B	−37.2%	63.3%
P. Pioneer HY; Class C	−37.4%	60.8%
Q. Fidelity Adv High IncAdvt; Class C	−39.5%	68.2%
R. John Hancock HY; Class B	−48.8%	68.4%
S. Highland High Income; Class C	−57.3%	—
T. Oppenheimer Chpn Inc; Class B	−78.7%	19.3%
Average	**−44.3%**	**49.5%**

Source: Lipper, a Thompson Reuters company. Used by permission.

NOTES

Introduction
1. Nomura Corporate Research and Asset Management, High Yield Total Return Institutional Composite (HYTRIC). Used by permission.
2. BoA Merrill Lynch High Yield Bond Indices. Used by permission.

Chapter 2
1. A prospectus for a new issue must contain all the relevant corporate information. Prospectuses are available for all public new issues. However, most new junk bonds are issued privately under Regulation 144A and are not available to individual investors. Those issues take some time, at least six months, for the 144A bonds to convert to public bonds, which are available to individual investors. For that reason, individual investors primarily look for seasoned bonds. Occasionally, a junk bond issue can be sold as a public offering and a prospectus is available.

Chapter 12
1. H0A0 used from 1992–1996; HUC0 used from 1996–2009.
2. The *pro forma* (PF) *leverage* is anticipated leverage before the fact. Because markets are forward looking, this can significantly move bond prices.

Chapter 15
1. Frank K. Reilly, David J. Wright, and James A. Gentry, "Historic Changes in the High Yield Bond Market," *Journal of Applied Corporate Finance*, Morgan Stanley, vol. 21, no. 3, 2009, pp. 65–79.

Chapter 19
1. *JPMorgan 2010 High Yield Annual Review*, pp. 41 and A55; plus December numbers, p. A57.
2. Ibid., pp. A74–A80.
3. Fortune 500 2010 Rankings.
4. "McKesson Corporation" in Wikipedia.

Chapter 20

1. Univision Communications, Inc., *Univision 2010 Third Quarter Results*, November 4, 2010.
2. LyondellBasell, "LyondellBasell: Polymers, Chemicals, Fuels, and Technology," About Us, http://www.lyondellbasell.com/Aboutus/.
3. Third amended disclosure statement accompanying third amended joint Chapter 11 plan of reorganization for the LyondellBasell debtors, March 12, 2010, p. 38; Andrew Ross Sorkin, *DealBook*, "Lyondell Files for Bankruptcy," NYTimes.com, *New York Times*, January 6, 2009.
4. Aleris International, About Aleris, http://www.aleris.com/about-aleris. Accessed February 7, 2011.
5. Christopher Witkowsky, "Apollo, Oaktree, Bain to Take over TPG's Aleris," *Private Equity International*, February 10, 2010, http://www.peimedia.com/Article.aspx?article=50525&hashID=A7B2F62B33EA82747E1700EBAF2AAE938DF574A1. Accessed February 7, 2011.

Chapter 21

1. http://www.oppenheimerfundfraud.com/.

Glossary

Basis point: 1/100 of 1%.

Corporate bankruptcy: When a company cannot meet its financial obligations, it files for protection under the U.S. bankruptcy law.

- **Chapter 7:** A company stops all operations and goes out of business. Creditors are paid off based on their place in the capital structure.
- **Chapter 11:** A company is allowed time through reorganization to return to normal business operations in the future. Generally, creditors are paid cents on the dollar based on their place within the capital structure. For example, secured lenders are higher in priority than unsecured lenders, and unsecured lenders are higher in priority than preferred and common stockholders.

Coupon: The interest payment on a debt security.

Current yield: The coupon of a debt security divided by its market price.

Debt leverage ratio: Debt divided by EBITDA.

Depreciation: A noncash charge that spreads out the cost of a tangible asset over its useful life. For example, a factory that costs $1 million could be depreciated over 10 years at $100,000 per year.

Derivative: An instrument whose market value ultimately depends on, or derives from, the value of a more fundamental investment vehicle called the *underlying asset* or *security*.

EBITDA: Earnings before interest, taxes, depreciation, and amortization.

EBITDA margin: EBITDA divided by revenue. Shows what percentage of revenue a company kept as EBITDA.

Exchange-traded fund (ETF): A managed investment fund that trades like a stock over an exchange. The two high yield ETFs are Barclays Capital High Yield Very Liquid Index (JNK) and iBoxx $ Liquid High Yield Index (HYG).

Fallen angel: A corporate bond that has been downgraded from investment grade to high yield.

Financial Industry Regulatory Authority (FINRA): The largest independent regulator of member firms and exchanges conducting business in the United States.

Gross margin: Gross profit divided by revenue. The gross margin shows what percentage of revenue a company has kept as gross profit.

Gross profit: Revenue minus the cost of goods sold.

High yield bond: A bond rated below investment grade (below BBB– by Standard & Poor's). High yield bonds are considered to be more risky and able to return higher yields than investment grade bonds. Also known as *Junk bonds* and *Speculative grade bonds*.

Institutional investor: An organization with large sums of money such as a pension fund, mutual fund, investment bank, or money manager. Some are allowed to trade unregistered securities.

Interest coverage ratio: EBITDA divided by annual interest expense.

Interest expense: The total interest payments a company pays to its bondholders. This figure is found on the income statement.

Investment grade bond: A bond rated BBB– and above by Standard & Poor's. Investment grade bonds are considered less risky and return a lower yield than high yield bonds.

Junk bond: see *High yield bond*.

Leveraged buyout (LBO): The acquisition of a company primarily funded with debt, where the debt repayment and service comes from the cash flow and cash of the acquired company.

Margin analysis: Comparing a company's margins (for example, EBITDA margin, gross margin) over time and against its competitors. This is calculated by dividing each of those numbers by revenue to yield a percent.

Operating income: The gross profit minus the selling, general, and administrative (SG&A) expenses.

Operating margin: The operating income divided by revenue. The operating margin shows what percentage of revenue a company has kept as operating income.

Option-adjusted spread (OAS): Essentially the spread between the relevant bond and its equivalent maturity Treasury.

Par bond: The par value, or principal value, of a high yield bond, which is generally stated as $1,000. Principal value is not the same as market value.

Prospectus: A public offering document filed with the SEC and available to investors. It should contain the relevant information for making an investment decision. A mutual fund prospectus should contain the fund objectives, investment restrictions, investment guidelines, and other relevant information.

Rating agency: The company that analyzes the creditworthiness of debt securities and then assigns them ratings (such as A–, BB, or CCC+). The three major rating agencies are Standard & Poor's, Moody's, and Fitch.

Regulation FD: All investors, individuals, and institutions should have equal access to company information. This regulation was adopted by the SEC in the year 2000.

Return on investment (ROI): (Ending value of investment – initial investment)/initial investment.

Rising star: A corporate bond upgraded from high yield to investment grade.

Risk-free rate: The interest rate that is assigned to investments that are theoretically free of risk because they are backed by the full faith and credit of the U.S. government. It is the rate of return on a three-month Treasury bill (T-bill).

Securities and Exchange Commission (SEC): Federal agency that oversees and enforces regulations regarding all registered securities and exchanges in the United States.

Selling, general, and administrative (SG&A) expenses: These could include costs of sales, marketing expenses, and operational costs. The SG&A expenses are found on the income statement.

Sharpe ratio: Used to calculate return per unit of risk.

Short investing: Selling a security with the hope of purchasing it back at a later date.

Small-cap growth fund: A category of mutual funds. Other categories could include large-cap funds. Small-cap funds typically invest in companies that have a smaller market value than mid-cap or large-cap funds. Generally they have higher growth than the others and more volatility.

Speculative grade bonds: See *High yield bonds.*

Spread: The difference in yield between the bond of interest and the equivalent maturity Treasury. Spreads are measured in basis points.

Strong-Horse Method: A credit analysis method. When relating it to pricing adequacy, it becomes an investment style.

T-bill: A Treasury bill—that is, a U.S. Treasury debt security that expires in one year or less.

Trade Reporting and Compliance Engine (TRACE): A FINRA-designed system that records and reports all secondary market debt securities transactions.

Volatility: The variability of an investment's returns. In this book, it is calculated as the standard deviation of returns. A larger number means a greater variation in returns.

Yield to call (YTC): A bond's annual return through its next call date at the call price.

Yield to maturity (YTM): A bond's annual return through maturity.

Yield to worst (YTW): A bond's lowest possible return considering the call schedule.

Index

About the Author

Robert Levine, CFA, left Nomura in 2010, after nearly 20 years. He served as the Nomura Corporate Research and Asset Management (NCRAM) president, chief executive officer, and chief investment officer since its founding in 1991.

Levine founded NCRAM as an analyst-driven, asset management boutique for debt that was rated as below investment grade. He was originally the portfolio manager for high yield debt and then served as the chief investment officer for all NCRAM portfolios. In those capacities, he led NCRAM into expansion in the areas of emerging market debt and syndicated bank debt.

Prior to his position at Nomura, Levine was with Kidder, Peabody & Company for 13 years, most recently as president of Kidder, Peabody High Yield Asset Management (KPHYAM). Earlier, he was a managing director of the Merchant Banking Department. He also founded the High Yield Department, for which he was the director of research. For that department, his publications included *The High Yield Sector Report*, which provided up-to-date analyses of the high yield market, focusing on portfolio strategy and bond selection.

Robert Levine is a CFA Charter Holder, and he is a past member of the Association for Investment Management and Research (AIMR) Accounting Policy Committee. Levine is a past director and past president of the Fixed Income Analysts Society, and he was recently inducted into that society's Hall of

Fame. He earned his MBA from the Wharton School of Finance and his undergraduate degree from The City College of New York. Levine was a student instructor in the MBA program at the Wharton School, and he has been an adjunct professor in the MBA program at the Stern School of Business at New York University.

Levine resides in Princeton, New Jersey, and he is married and has three children. He is on the board of directors of the New York State Teachers Pension Fund Investment Advising Committee as well as several community and religious organizations.